A COMMON
MAN'S VOICE

BE THE DIFFERENCE!

ROBERT MARKS

FIRST EDITION

Marks, Robert

A Common Man's Voice / Robert Marks – 1st ed.

0^6 1^8 2^1 3^1 4^2 5^5 6^6 7^2 8^1 9^2

ISBN: 978-0-692-92142-5

An Imprint of HamiltonDickinson

Dedication

This humble effort, as my humble existence, is lovingly dedicated to my high school sweetheart and love of my life. Thank you for joining me on this wonderful, joyful, and everlasting journey. For lifting me up, raising our family, laughing at my snarky jokes, and generally making me a better person; you are my heart, my happiness, my life.

I also want to dedicate this to my two beautiful children, who are both in college pursuing inspiring dreams of their own. My daughter, who undoubtedly will be the kindest, gentlest, most motivating elementary teacher ever, and my son, who is doggedly trying to unravel the most complicated human diseases including HIV; I am so very proud of both of you. I love you with all my heart. America is indeed in good hands with your generation.

Contents

A COMMON
MAN'S VOICE
BE THE DIFFERENCE!

Robert Marks

Forward:
A Common Man

There is simply nothing remarkable about me, beyond my beautiful family; my eternal soul mate of 30+ years and two incredible children. Yes I understand that every person's family is beautiful, so again I am utterly unremarkable even in this regard. I am about as "common" as one can get. At times in my life I have succeeded, at times I have utterly failed; mostly I have stammered aimlessly through the great mediocrity of my existence and a comfortable middle-class life. I am convinced that there is nothing special, gifted, or unique here. At fifty-three, a li'l pudgy, and balding, I am little more than a piece of dry plain toast on a Monday morning; quintessentially bland & boring. They even call me "Tubbs", whether I want them to or not.

While I am a common man, I'm more than a little fed up with both the Republican and Democratic parties today. Both parties try to cater to the loud-mouthed, vocal extremist within their parties, ignoring the vast majority of citizens who are moderate and in the middle of the political spectrum. You know, the folks that schlepp to work every day, go to church on Sunday, celebrate the 4th of July, and pay their taxes timely. I truly believe that 10% of our population is ultra-right wing, nationalist, fascist, homophobes and another 10% are left wing liberals, "friend of them long haired, hippie-type, pinkos". That leaves the remaining 80% of our citizens in what I believe is "true" America, moderate with some variations leaning both conservative on some issues and some leaning liberal on other issues, but overall pretty moderate. The ocean of 80% is simply the common folks struggling through life in America, while trying to take care of their loved ones. These are the important people we should be focused on not the extremist pushing their radical agendas on either side.

I have always considered myself to be a true independent, not because of some altruistic desire to avoid sensitive political arguments. You'll find out soon enough, I love a good argument no matter the topic (my apologies, mama). While I consider myself an independent, for the record I have registered at different times in my life as both Republican and Democrat, mostly for the convenience of voting in the local primaries. I literally have no political allegiance. Undoubtedly the political parties, media pundits, and pollsters hate people like me; much to my amusement and enjoyment. Regardless of which political camp I temporarily hung my hat in over the years, I have voted for both Republicans and Democratic presidential candidates throughout my lifetime. I've always done my very best to learn the issues research the candidates and vote for who I thought was gonna be the best president without consideration of race, religion, or sex. I am a practical pragmatist and I abhor preachy, self-righteous, small-minded, non-intellectual ideologues.

With all of that on the table, I am sitting down today to write out my thoughts on a few topics facing America. Not as a left wing or right wing partisan, just as an American; an insignificant common man, nothing more. It is not my goal to convince anyone that my positions are right, but rather simply to say these are my positions. While you may not agree with me, please know that I do respect your position, though my rhetoric may not always show it. I am certain that some folks will take issue with almost every single one of my thoughts, one way or the other. Heck that's America; I wouldn't have any other way.

You may agree with some of my positions, while others you'll be fit to be tied and spitting bullets, and that's okay. What I am trying to accomplish here is while folks might not agree with me on a given topic, they may be prompted to ask themselves what their heartfelt position is regarding the topic. In doing so, we would have opened a dialogue, a worthy goal. After all, collectively "We the people" own this great nation, our future, and our destiny. It's about high time we began speaking to one another, neighbor to neighbor, without political parties, or the vail of political-correctness standing in the way.

Each of us comes from different backgrounds, upbringings, faiths, morals, and experiences with the single common thread being our humanity. It is little wonder that we will have different positions on different topics. My hope is that we can view these differences with respect and reverence, not demonization. I will do my best to not reference any American politician. I don't want the conversation to be lost in political vitriol. I promise not to pull any punches. I am pretty opinionated and don't mince words, apologies in advance.

I want all Americans to set aside our petty squabbles with one another and accept that we are all flesh and bone. Instead of pointless screaming at one another, perhaps we could defend and protect each other's rights, as we would our own family. We should trust that other Americans will protect each of our rights in return. We should open our hearts and minds to become a more compassionate, tolerant, and caring America for all.

Abortion

Did I mention that I was opinionated? Currently, we have two sides locked in a passion fueled intractable argument over Abortion. Both sides are convinced they are right and the other side is absolutely wrong. Problem here is that neither side is actually talking to the other side about their common positions. Instead they hysterically scream their position towards the other side in the hopes of drowning out any reasonable argument. We desperately need civility in this debate.

On one side, the Pro-lifers say absolutely no abortion is acceptable; no woman should ever have a choice, regardless of the specific circumstances. They view human life beginning at the moment of conception and any abortion would equate to no less than murder. Pro-lifers are horrified with *Roe v. Wade*, seeking to overturn the law of the land while interjecting their own sense of self-determined, righteous morality regarding abortion on everyone else.

Abortion

On the other side, we have the Pro-choice group that says make up your own mind and let your conscience be your guide, consistent with your faith, moral upbringing, and unique circumstances. Pro-choice recognizes that every individual comes from a different moral compass and every circumstance is unique. Specifically, Pro-choice argues that the woman is in the very best position to determine the fate for herself and her fetus.

The current abortion argument is frustrating to me as neither side can see the rationale of the other. With only two sides arguing, they both appear to be philosophically and absolutely opposed. While this is the outward appearance, it frankly is not the truth. Beyond the hysterical rants of "murderer" and "baby-killer", which are inflammatory and misplaced, in reality the diametrically opposite position of Pro-life is not Pro-choice, but rather Pro-abortion.

Thank goodness a Pro-abortion group calling for the immediate termination of every pregnancy does not exist today in America. However, given the extreme position of the Pro-lifers who believe no abortion is acceptable, I am fascinated another such extremist group calling for the immediate abortion of every fetus doesn't already exist. Today we have a group, the Pro-lifers, that say absolutely no abortion should ever be permitted regardless of medical necessity or circumstances. That is an incredibly extremist and narrow minded view. I submit that this extremist view is no more ridiculous or absurd than the opposite extremist view that every pregnancy should be aborted immediately upon detection of the fetus.

Without a doubt every decision by a woman to either carry a fetus to term or to abort is absolutely gut-wrenching and soul searching for the woman. There is simply no single being closer to the fetus than the woman herself. Accordingly there is no one, certainly not the government, in a better position than her to make such an important decision about what is best for her or her fetus. Everyone else who is not the pregnant woman regarding this issue, should respect and support her decision, shut-up, and go home. And dads to-be, this includes y'all too. I understand you donated some sperm to this little party. However in my opinion, you are not a father until the umbilical cord is cut and the fetus is no longer attached or dependent on the host mother.

While I whole heartedly believe that pro-choice is the only rational and logical position in this debate, personally I believe this freedom of choice should only be exercised in the first two trimesters of pregnancy. I believe that six months is sufficient time to make such an important decision. I would however qualify that position with the single exception; if the life of the mother is determined to be medically in jeopardy during the last trimester by two attending physicians then abortion would still be a viable option. Otherwise this would constitute a potential death sentence for the mother, who is guilty of no crime against society.

The issue we have in resolving the abortion debate in America is not reconciling the differing positions. Again the Pro-choice position certainly allows for a woman to carry the fetus to term based on her unique circumstances, moral and religious convictions, and choice. So the Pro-choice position itself is sufficient to accommodate a Pro-life woman's choice and beliefs to not have an abortion. Rest assured, no one in America is ever going to force an unwanted abortion nor should they.

The fundamental issue we have today in resolving the abortion debate is at best contrived by a very vocal minority. Though well-intentioned, misguided Pro-lifers are trying to hoist and impose their personal religious and moral views on the rest of society, who frankly may or may not hold the same views on either religion or morality. These folks should allow people to live their own lives. And anyone who "thinks" they are doing GOD's work to bomb abortion clinics, assault medical staff, or deny access are NOT Christians but rather domestic terrorist!

Child Marriage

Really, children allowed to get married in the United States? I seriously can't believe this topic is even up for debate. Are we a civilized society or a backwards, third world nation? The very notion is vile, disgusting, and exploitative to me. The US Department of State defines Child Marriage as:

"A formal marriage or informal union where one or both parties is under the age of 18."

The states regulate and set the permissible age for marriage within their respective borders and clearly are doing a piss poor job at it. I believe the federal government needs to step in and establish a reasonable and uniform age for marriage across the United States. All but two states have established eighteen as the legal age for marriage. The two exceptions are Nebraska at nineteen and Mississippi at twenty-one. If the state legislators had left well enough alone with this and allowed these ages for marriage to stand, there simply wouldn't be child marriage in the United States today and we wouldn't be having this silly conversation.

Of course you know the story by now, the state legislators couldn't leave well enough alone and added what I consider to be *"pervert clauses and exceptions"* to the permissible age for marriage in their state. Unbelievably twenty-seven states have NO minimum age for marriage at all providing other statutory requirements are met. This means a child as young as twelve could be and have been married. Another twenty-two states permit marriages under eighteen with the youngest permissible age being New Hampshire at thirteen. ONLY New York has very recently established the minimum age of marriage at eighteen. Hopefully ALL states will soon follow New York's leadership on this topic.

Before folks get upset at me that young lovers should be allowed to wed into marital bliss, understand we ain't talking about Romeo and Juliet here. What we are talking about is very young prepubescent children being sexually assaulted and raped by much older perverts and pedophiles. Can I be more blunt in my assessment? ANY state which permits child marriage is unwittingly aiding, assisting, and abetting rapist, pedophiles, and perverts. Some of these state laws date back to the mid-1800's when average life expectancy was little more than thirty-eight years old. This is precisely the argument that many supporters (State Legislators) of child rape offer; "the law has been on the books for over a hundred years, why change it now?" Here is one obvious observation. Today life expectancy in the United States is around eighty years old. There is no urgency from a life expectancy perspective to permit child marriages.

Other supporters of child marriage would argue that young children may become pregnant either via rape or unlawful consent. While certainly an unsettling fact, I still can't make the connection to "why" we would permit child marriage. Two wrongs certainly don't make a right. If the young girl is pregnant by either rape or unlawful consent, than she has a very difficult and unenviable choice to make a) carry to term to either raise the child or place for adoption or b) have an abortion. She should be supported and nurtured, regardless of her choice.

Children under eighteen should not be allowed to marry, period! Certainly a twelve or thirteen year old child should never be allowed to marry. All are too young. To me this is painfully obvious, if a child is too young to vote, too young to drive a car, too young to get a credit card, or too young to serve in the military than by golly they are likewise too young to be married.

Corporations

I must've dozed off during Sunday school that hot summer's day when they taught that GOD created corporations in HIS image. Obviously, this is far-fetched. But you wouldn't know that if you talk to any of the Wall Street boys. They literally believe corporations are living beings with the same rights as humans. Hogwash!

This is utterly ridiculous to me. Corporations have no more rights than a toaster, a TV set, or a bicycle. These are all inanimate objects created by man. Humans have rights, animals have rights, and I could possibly even be convinced that plants have rights. However, corporations have no rights whatsoever.

The issue we see today is Corporations wield way too much power in America and they think that they are entitled to do so by their supposed "rights". The problem is the more power corporations wield; the less power that every day Americans citizens can legitimately exercise. If you were a Congressman or

Senator, who are ya gonna listen to Exxon/Mobil or Joe Smith (Hicksville, Ohio). I believe our elected officials across America need to start listening to Joe Smith.

The only reason corporations exist is as a legal entity which limits investor's personal liabilities and facilitates accumulation of capital. Corporations are not citizens, cannot vote, nor are they guaranteed freedom of speech. However, they do have huge buckets of cash and certainly are more than willing to grease a few squeaky wheels for favorable legislation; whether it is fracking in Oklahoma or drilling on National Wildlife Parks. We need to get corporations and their huge buckets of cash out of influencing our American democracy. I very much want to reduce corporations in America back to their original intent that of an investment vehicle and NOTHING more.

There are several measures we can do to help reduce the influence that corporations have on the American political landscape. As I mentioned, corporations have no guaranteed freedom of speech and cannot vote. We need to proactively distance corporations and their ever present bucket of cash from our political system; blocking them from our elected officials on all levels of government and eliminate their octopian influence.

Corporations should be prohibited from making direct contributions to political parties, campaigns, and candidates.

Corporations

Likewise corporations should be prevented from contributing directly to political action committees, as well. Corporations simply should not be permitted to participate in the election process. Shareholders have their own voice. Perhaps the most important element that we need to restrict from corporations is the ability to hire political lobbyists to continually push their agenda and cajole elected officials with gifts. Unfortunately, both political parties and elected officials too often consider corporations to be their defacto constituents, affording more credence and gravitas to the corporation lobbyist than an ordinary voter from their home district. After all, the ordinary voter isn't likely to donate substantial monies to their re-election campaign. In Washington D.C., "Money talks... Bologna walks". I have no issue if corporations proactively market their products for sale. But our American democracy is not for sale.

The last element we need to address with corporations is favorable tax treatment. This is true across the board whether it is federal taxes or local taxes we are speaking about. Our tax codes have been created with corporate loopholes in place which must be closed. Also local municipalities are guilty of providing reduced or even exempted local taxes to corporations to entice moving to their district. Both practices need to stop immediately, as citizens are not granted the same consideration.

14

Robert Marks

Criminal Justice

Ok let's count noses, who is left after the Abortion conversation? Can you tell I am a grumpy old man? Let's plow ahead. I am very much in favor of the rule of law. Specifically, I believe that all members of society benefit by codified rules of coexistence. These rules of coexistence must be enforced to establish a fair and level playing field for all members of society to flourish. It is more than troubling, that too often in our pursuit of enforcement of these societal safeguards, we slip into our own human foibles, prejudices, and vulnerabilities. Too often today our police enforcement, especially when dealing with minorities, appears to be racially discriminatory, biased, and unduly confrontational.

As a society, we must address this apparent biasness with additional rigorous training, counseling, strengthening hiring qualifications, body cameras, and continual psychological evaluations. Police enforcement has to be balanced, fact based, and even-handed with a blind eye to preferences or prejudice. We have to take proactive measures to improve the current policing environment and community trust. While this is true, we cannot on the other hand besiege our police as an enemy or preempt their enforcement of these laws. They are serving society. In doing so, they routinely place themselves in danger and direct harm. Make no mistake, being a Police Officer is one of the most difficult jobs in America. Both our communities and Police departments need to repair this relationship and trust.

Regarding capital punishment, currently there are forty-one Federal Capital offences. Thirty-One of these offences deal directly with Murder, eight more offences deal with nefarious acts resulting in death including genocide, and the remaining two offences address both Treason and Espionage against the United States. I have to say for these types of horrendous crimes against society, I am a supporter of capital punishment. This is a very difficult topic for me, as I am sure it is for everyone across our nation. But in my heart, I simply do not believe there is a debt sufficient to pay society for these types of horrific crimes other than the ultimate debt of life.

Certainly without a doubt, we should have reasonable and exhaustive safeguards in place to ensure that an innocent person is not convicted or punished. However when there is overwhelming evidence, which can uniquely identify the perpetrator with certainty, I believe capital punishment is appropriate and a measured remedy to remove a threat from our society. Note I said "remove" not "rehabilitate". I know some folks will undoubtedly toss out the 8th Amendment:

> *"Excessive bail shall not be required, nor excessive fines imposed, nor cruel and unusual punishment inflicted."*

These folks would likely argue about what constitutes "cruel and unusual punishment." Fair enough. I would counter that argument with "whatever means the convicted murderer dispatched their victims" would be acceptable by the 8th Amendment standards. Clearly it cannot be seen as "unusual" because the convicted murderer did it before to the victim, nothing unusual about it. Nor could it be considered particularly cruel by the murderer because again they applied the same technique to their victim. This approach would reconcile the 8th amendment, I feel better now.

While applying the same technique to the murderer that they applied to their victim is one approach, it's simply not practical. If we are going to have Capital Punishment on the books for horrendous crimes, then it is incumbent upon us to ensure the most humane method possible to effect the punishment. However, when convicted with clear and irrefutable evidence, this sentence should be carried out with within three years of the original conviction. To accomplish this, we would need to improve the speed of legitimate appeals, but this process should not be perpetual and never ending. Too often today, we permit these horrible human beings to outlive their victims by 20+ years. This inflicts unbearable pain on the survivors and is frankly unconscionable.

Beyond crimes fit for Capital Punishment, there is another crime we need to discuss which is too often overlooked today that demands stronger sentencing. These criminals destroy thousands of lives, families, relationships, homes, retirements, and futures. Even so, they seldom get more than a slap on the wrist and often face no jail time whatsoever.

These are the white-collar criminals. Whether they are predatory lenders running mortgage scams, bankers fraudulently opening accounts, CEOs cooking multiple sets of books, or self-professed investment gurus selling the latest snake oil Ponzi scheme (thank you Bernie M!); these are awful human beings and leaches on Society, who have ruined thousands of lives. We should aggressively pursue these individuals with mandatory minimum sentencing for convictions of no less than one year prison for each victim of their crimes. I see no difference between thieves breaking into your home to steal thousands of dollars or a white-collar criminal cowardly doing the same thing from the anonymity and safety of their high rise corner office. A crook is a crook.

While I am a supporter of both capital punishment for horrendous crimes and rightfully punishing white-collar criminals who've left a wake of destruction in their path, I believe we have to reevaluate the use of mandatory minimum sentencing for lower-level victimless crimes. Whether the crime is possession of a negligible amount of a controlled substance or another lesser crime; I don't believe that mandating minimum sentences for these lesser crimes serves society well. For example a person convicted of possessing (1) gram of LSD faces a mandatory minimum sentence of (5) years while an individual who possesses (0.9) gram of LSD faces no minimum sentence. To me this appears a bit extreme from a sentencing perspective. With just a tiny fraction more of a controlled substance, we as a society are willing to take away five years of an individual's life.

When I say this doesn't serve society well, there are several factors in play. Firstly it is extremely expensive to incarcerate an individual costing taxpayers almost $30,000 yearly per inmate. Our earlier example will cost taxpayers an additional $150,000 for a person in possession of (0.1) gram more of LSD. In addition to the direct costs of incarcerating a prisoner, there are often additional indirect costs to the taxpayers in the form of welfare, food stamps, and housing to support the families affected by an incarceration. Beyond the simple dollars and cents associated with incarceration, there is an enormous social cost also realized. An individual, who wrongly endures five years in prison for a minor offense, will likely come out of prison with an understandable grievance against society; which may manifest in more serious crimes being pursued. On a more personal level, we are needlessly tearing apart families. For these lower-level offenses, I believe society is better served if the time actually matches the crime.

Along these lines of re-evaluating our handling of lesser and victimless crimes, we need to legalize two issues which needlessly clog our courts and prisons at considerable taxpayer cost. The first issue we should legalize is drinking at eighteen years old. The current drinking age of twenty-one is more than a little arbitrary. At eighteen years old we consider an individual to be an adult with the right to vote, serve in our military, and purchase a gun. Yet, these same individuals are not allowed to buy a beer? Why? This makes no sense to me. Frankly, it smacks of age discrimination and latter-day prohibition.

The next issue we need to address is the legalization of Marijuana, which is far less addictive and harmful than either alcohol or tobacco. Personally, I don't use marijuana. Even so I see no reason for this to be illegal. I have heard the arguments that marijuana is a gateway drug. As I mentioned, Marijuana has limited if any addictive properties, certainly not to the degree of either alcohol or tobacco. So marijuana itself is not a gateway drug, no more so than alcohol or tobacco. However, I will concede that today dubious drug dealers will lace marijuana with far more addictive substances like PCP (Phencyclidine), aka Angel Dust. The drug dealers do this in the hopes of hooking their customers and creating a chemical dependency for more expensive and dangerous narcotics.

Given that Marijuana is no more dangerous or addictive than alcohol or tobacco, if we legalize it, we accomplish several beneficial and desirable outcomes for society. First off by legalizing marijuana, we deny drug dealers of their all-important customers and cash flow. More importantly, we prevent drug dealers the possibility of lacing marijuana with more addictive substances to induce a chemical dependency. With legalization we can regulate and oversee the product to ensure addictive elements are not introduced. Also once fully legalized, we could raise revenues by taxing it as we do alcohol and tobacco. Lastly this would lessen the burden on our judicial system and police enforcement allowing both to focus on more serious crimes against society.

The last issue I would like to touch on regarding criminal justice is reintegration back into our society after the individual has fully paid their debt to society and successfully served their time. Unfortunately, we have some very vindictive individuals in our country that believe former felons should be punished for life, well beyond their original sentencing. I don't agree with this notion. I believe once a debt to society is paid, the individual should be fully reintegrated into our community. In doing so, the individual has a vested interest in society succeeding. To deny a former felon their rights after they have served their time is to deny their American citizenship. Please understand, we cannot have two or more classes of citizenship in our country, where some citizens are worthy of rights while other citizens are determined to be unworthy of the same rights. This approach certainly failed miserably with immoral slavery and denying women's right to vote. If you are an American citizen, your rights are guaranteed and must be aggressively protected.

One very egregious area where former felons are disenfranchised from their constitutional rights is the right to vote. Various states, for purely political purposes, have crafted laws which deny prior felons of their constitutional right to vote. The worst of these is Florida, a bell weather swing state. Before you dismiss the fact that denying former felons their constitutionally guaranteed right to vote is a major problem, understand that this affects approximately 2.5% of our voting age population in the United States. This translates to roughly six million American citizens currently being denied their Constitutional rights. Florida are you proud of yourself?

As I mentioned earlier, I'm a strong supporter of both rule of law and capital punishment. If an individual commits a crime then by all means they should be punished as prescribed by law, but not beyond that. Denying American citizens their rights after they have paid their debt to society isn't a question of being soft on crime or not. This is a question of right and wrong. You either believe that America is the greatest country in the world and ALL our citizens are granted equal rights or you don't. There is no middle ground here. We simply cannot be guilty as Americans to say "blue-eyed folks are granted these rights, while brown eyed folks only get these rights". I fervently believe that denying former felons their basic American rights violates our Constitution. Accordingly, I would like to see the US Supreme Court strike down these heinous, politically motivated state laws as unconstitutional.

Democracy

Perhaps the venerable Prime Minister of Great Britain Sir Winston Churchill said it best,

> *"Indeed it has been said that democracy is the worst form of Government except for all those other forms that have been tried from time to time"*.

I couldn't agree more with Churchill's quip. We are truly blessed in America with our Democracy, as well as, our freedoms and rights. Nonetheless, we still have room for improvement.

I believe in the concept of a "true democracy"; one man, one woman, one vote (and the heavenly choir breaks into angelic song, as harps strum melodiously). Now, ask yourself when is the last time you voted for the President of the United States? Frankly, the answer is never. That may surprise folks, but it's a fact. We cast our votes for Senators, Congress, Governors, City

Councils, School Boards, and even the lonely Dog-Catcher in some districts. Strangely, we do not vote for the most important office in the land, either the President or Vice President for that matter.

You can blame Alexander Hamilton (*Federalist No. 68*) and our founding fathers for this fiasco (*see US Constitution Article II, Section 1, Clause 3 and the 12th Amendment*). I know, I love the musical too! And yes, Lin-Manuel Miranda is indeed a genius. Even so, Hamilton really blew this one. His plan called for citizens to vote for an electoral-college representative, who in turn cast their vote for the President of the United States of America. Citizens of the United States have literally never actually voted for their President.

This is certainly a curious fact in such a proud Democracy as ours; and a fact that is not too well understood by our citizens. People find this fact unsettling and very confusing because when they go to vote at the local Elementary's Café-Gym-atorium the presidential candidate's name is present on the ballot and the voter marks it accordingly. We "assume" that we have voted for the President. That of course is a groundless, baseless, and far-fetched assumption. In reality what is happening is you are casting your vote for an Electoral College representative, who pledges to vote the way you voted. The problem with this system is in many states the Electoral College Representatives are not obligated to do so. And in other States its winner take all, meaning your represented-vote for President cast by the Electoral Voter, may in fact be cast for the opponent from the other political party. That stinks doesn't it? The common vote of our citizens is cast as the "Popular Vote", which is entirely non-binding (that and a quarter will get ya a cup of coffee). Only the vote of the Electoral College members determines the President. Citizens have no say, whatsoever.

Now there are many reasons, rationales, and justifications for why the Electoral College was originally created by our founding fathers. Some say the Electoral College was to serve as a check and balance to the opinions of the masses, the electorate. While others legitimate that it was simply impossible to count four million votes (our population) by hand in the late 1700's across a large geographically dispersed country. Still others contend that voters would not have received adequate or sufficient electoral information to adequately inform their judgment, as pony express was the most efficient and reliable means of transmission of information back then.

As far as, a "check and balance" on the voters, I call horse hockey on that. The voters don't need or want a virtual vote-nanny sitting over our shoulders, changing our intended votes.

The other arguments, counting millions of votes by hand and efficient dissemination of information makes more sense to me, especially in the 1700's before computers and the speed of the internet. Nowadays we can actually find out the popular vote, as soon as, we can learn the Electoral College votes if not sooner. And anyone who has endured months of mind-numbing political attack ads, robo-calls, radio spots, emails, text messages, or banner ads on the internet can attest that access to political information is no longer an issue. Why do we still have this anachronism from the 1700's when it is no longer needed and has outlived its useful life? I suspect very few folks today dawn a horse-whip or spurs simply to take a car ride to the grocery store. Though in history, both items were useful. They are simply not needed today, nor is the Electoral College.

In the United States only (538) people officially vote for the President. These are the members of the Electoral College. The formula of how they came up with (538) is straightforward enough, though easily argued both pro/con. Each State gets (2) members for the number of US Senators the state has plus a number of members equal to the US Congressmen the state has allocated. In addition to these Electoral College Members, (3) members are provided for the District of Columbia, which is not a state but granted under the 23rd Amendment. Add it all up and *voilà*, you get (538) Electoral College Voters. By the way, "shhhh" please don't tell the folks in Puerto Rico, Guam, U.S. Virgin Islands or any other US territory that they literally have no Electoral College representation whatsoever. It will be our little secret.

Not surprisingly, the Constitution does not specify minimal qualifications to serve as a member of the Electoral College. There are a few "don't(s)" that are attached to the job description, but nothing that is earth shattering. The members of the Electoral College are appointed by the various State Legislatures. You can imagine it takes some pretty good ass-kissin' to get on the list of (538) folks whose vote for President actually counts. The process is wrought with political favors, gamesmanship, and party self-interest. Not exactly the way I would choose the most important office in America. And for the really skeptical among us, we have to remember it's of course easier to pay off with bribes or favors (538) folks instead of nearly (130) million citizens who cast their popular vote in 2016.

Simply put, the Electoral College has outlived its purpose and should quietly go the way of the dodo bird. On no less than (5) different elections (1824 John Quincy Adams, 1876 Rutherford Hays, 1888 Benjamin Harris, 2000 George Bush, and 2016 Donald Trump) in our history the President officially elected by the Electoral College members, did not have the most votes of our citizens. Interestingly enough we have had (57) Presidential elections since 1788, which means the Electoral College has literally screwed up almost 9% of our Presidential Elections. Don't we deserve a more accurate process?

Dear (538), thanks but no thanks. I have more confidence in the men and women of our country to elect our President. Unfortunately, we can't unravel this mess without a Constitutional Amendment eliminating the Electoral College and establishing that the direct vote of our citizens will determine the President of the United States. This is long overdue especially in our Democracy and we need real leadership to affect this change; not the usual political lip-service. Ensuring that every citizen's vote actually counts in the Presidential Election is of extreme importance and is in the best interest of all citizens. Unless you prefer the current system where your vote does not count at all and you have no say whatsoever, I would encourage all citizens to demand the elimination of the Electoral College.

Education

Boy do we have our priorities screwed up on this one in America. Nothing more clearly illustrates this than the fact that starting quarterbacks in the NFL often make $5 million a year while a starting teacher in an elementary might be lucky to make $40,000 a year. The quarterbacks perform no meaningful benefit to society whatsoever other than throwing a pass or barking signals, while the teachers are literally forming our very future in their hands. The type of world we ultimately will live in is largely up to the skill, dedication, and tireless efforts of our teachers. They should be rewarded and paid accordingly. Personally, I don't care if they can throw a football or not!

Let me climb down from my teacher soap-box so we can continue. I have heard a lot of grumpy malcontents in the community, belly ache that they shouldn't have to pay school taxes because they have no kids attending school. Whenever a school bond or levy is up for a vote, these folks are standing on top of their rooftop screaming "Taxed Enough Already!" Now I am certainly not saying that every school bond or levy should be rubberstamped and automatically approved by the voters, as there's real money at stake. We will talk about that more here in a bit. What I am saying about school taxes for public education is that it is everyone's responsibility within our society to ensure equal and adequate education is available to everyone. This is simply part of living in the community; whether its public libraries, transportation, roads and highways, the post office, or the military all of these benefit our society as a whole. So too, does education.

While I believe it is everyone's responsibility to contribute to a sound and strong public education system, I do not believe that public monies should be siphoned away to endow private charter schools. I have nothing against charter schools. If someone believes that the world is flat, was created 6,000 years ago, dinosaurs never existed, and evolution never occurred than I say more power to you. I don't believe any of these, but if you do that's good enough for me. And if you're more comfortable sending your children to a private or charter school which teaches such silly horse manure, I have no problem with that either and will defend your right to do it.

Education

However, this should be paid out of <u>your</u> pocket, not the public purse. Permitting tax vouchers for charter or private schools tuition, is little more than public larceny. I understand that there are some excellent charter & private schools out there. On the other hand, there are some very poor public schools in certain areas. But this does not mean that we do not have a responsibility and obligation for improving the public schools to ensure everyone has a fair and equal opportunity to the future regardless of their race, ethnicity, or social status. And simply because the public school may not be up to par, this does not justify bleeding limited dollars away from the public system to enrich either a charter or private school. We are doing society an unconscionable disservice if we do this.

While I support public education and the responsibility that each of us have to fund it, too often we are guilty of squandering precious public funds. This is where some of those grumpy folks screaming from the roof-tops that I mentioned earlier actually have a valid point. When school bonds and levies are put forth for self-indulging monuments to our community egos and not for true educational purposes, I have a profound problem with that. It is not uncommon today to see a high school with a large new football stadium complete with artificial turf at a cost of millions and millions of dollars to the taxpayers. Horse-feathers!

For example, it has been reported that Allen High School's Eagle Stadium in Allen, TX cost a whopping $70 million and can seat nearly 18,000 fans for a High School game no less! This is in a community that only has 90,000 total citizens. How many math books, science labs, libraries, or computers could that $70 million have purchased? Sadly, likely not a penny of that $70 million went to true educational needs, it was all done to stroke the community's collective ego. And yes I grew up in Texas, so I do understand Texas football.

There are numerous other examples of this community ego stroking throughout our country, well beyond Texas. Even here in Southwest Ohio, it is quite common for each high school to have a brand new football stadium with artificial turf. Now before you say that I don't understand the importance of football to the community, as I mentioned I grew up in Texas playing football throughout my childhood. And even then, many-many years ago, football was nearly a second religion in Texas. I really do get it. Nonetheless my high school in Dallas, which actually won the coveted 5A State Championship, shared our old bleacher football field with another local high school and we played on grass not artificial turf. More often than not the grass was worn out midseason through, so we played on sun cracked dirt stirring up a looming cloud of dust on every play. Nobody complained.

I truly do not comprehend why a community would waste $70 million, so kids could play football. When that same $70 million could've paid for 1,750 teacher's salary for one year. They should be ashamed of themselves. Our priorities are clearly screwed up. And I would never support a school bond or levy that was not expressly dedicated to true educational needs.

Let's move on. Standardized tests are usually a very sore subject. Folks have very different views on the importance of standardized testing. I don't necessarily believe that any single test can assess a student's knowledge or command of the subject. Standardized Tests are often wrought with contrived bias or prejudices. This is incredibly unfair and sad. Even so I believe standardized tests are nearly the only vehicle we have to ensure a reasonable educational level has been achieved by all of our students. Equally important the standardized test provides a yardstick to measure school to school comparables.

While standardized test, when designed fairly without bias, have a place in our educational system, they unto themselves are not the end-all be-all of our education system nor should they be. Too often schools and parents alike become hyper focused on the administration of these tests and securing the best possible score for their student population. We've even had some school districts where administrators have "gamed" the system in the hopes of achieving higher test results. This is not only unethical but frankly disgraceful and sad.

There are many ways to reach, teach, and inspire students to learn and grow. Teachers and not administrators or Boards are in the very best position to challenge our students to realize their full potential. Teachers should have the freedom to explore which techniques are most beneficial for their unique student population. Teachers in the inner-city may find one technique is received better by their students, while teachers in rural communities may have a completely different experience. We have to remember that students and communities they come from are as diverse as the stars in the universe. There is no one single formula, which could be adequately or appropriately applied. In Education, one size does not fit all, nor should it.

From a funding perspective, I would gut Athletic budgets across the board. This expense is an indulgence not a necessity. Somebody else will need to validate these statistics, but I understand less than 1% of high school football players go pro and only 2% of college football players ultimately play in the pros. If the statistics are accurate what the heck are we wasting millions of dollars on? I would take that money from the athletic budget and invest it directly in building out STEM (Science, Technology, Engineering, and Mathematics) in our high schools. Another worthy educational expenditure above athletics is the arts, whether language arts or performance arts. Both of these are more valuable to society than athletics.

Let's focus a little bit on college affordability. Something is grossly wrong if students and families have to go into significant debt simply to achieve a college education. This does not advance our society. In fact it holds our society back from potential advancements. College educations must be affordable and accessible to everyone. There are several reasons why college educations are neither affordable nor accessible.

Perhaps one of the most material reasons why colleges are not affordable is the current endowment system. Colleges and universities both private and public are sitting on enormous endowment funds. These are funds that they've received in excess of their expenses, have been donated, or were made on other investments. Endowment funds are designed to guarantee the ongoing existence of the specific university.

Many universities in America are literally sitting on mountains of cash well beyond what they need to guarantee their future existence. It has been reported that Harvard has nearly $40 billion in endowments. Stanford University has over $20 billion, and both University of Pennsylvania and Texas A&M University each have nearly $10 billion in endowments. Endowments are indeed a weird animal within universities. They will continue to grow year after year protected by their regents, almost like a mad squirrel stocking away an inordinate amount of acorns for the winter and they are seldom if ever touched.

To help with the affordability of colleges, I believe we should limit and cap how large a university endowment can become. This should be based off of a reasonable ratio to their annual enrollment. Simply stated the more students are enrolled in the University, the larger their endowment can be, however, no endowment will exceed the calculated maximum permitted for any University. The excess above the maximum allowed endowment would be turned over to the Department of Education to reduce the tuition cost for all students seeking a college education via grants. This is one way that we can reduce the cost of college and ensure the affordability for all.

Environment

I have personally never been more embarrassed or infuriated with the United States than our recent snubbing of the historic Paris Climate Accord. The US literally looks like leaderless, arrogant, ignorant buffoons to the rest of the world. The accord was the first broad-based multilateral agreement, which addressed global climate change; specifically targeting reduction of greenhouse gases and rising global temperatures.

Incredibly (194) independent countries across the world all agreed and support the Paris Accord. There are only three countries in the world today that do not recognize the importance of climate change. Originally only Syria and Nicaragua refused to support the Paris agreement. These two admittedly backward countries were recently joined by none other than the United States of America. I can only surmise that America aspires to be as backward as both Syria and Nicaragua.

The United States refusal to acknowledge the reality of climate change is frankly incomprehensible. Global climate change is an irrefutable fact. The earth is currently getting warmer, which could have dire consequences to both the environment and humanity. We're only talking a few degrees of global warming since the industrial age began. However those few degrees will cause the polar icecaps to melt, which are already beginning to take place. The melting ice caps will greatly increase the ocean levels making many coastal areas simply uninhabitable (e.g. Florida). In addition, global rising temperatures are creating more violent storms and with a greater frequency than ever witnessed before. These storms are destroying both lives and property around the world.

The greenhouse effect, which is causing global warming, is relatively simple to understand. Concentrated levels of certain gases in our atmosphere traps excessive heat from the sun. The gases in effect act as a virtual greenhouse to the earth and rises temperatures as any greenhouse would do. CO_2 (carbon dioxide) is the principal gas which is contributing to the greenhouse effect. CO_2 gas is generated during the combustion of fossil fuels (coal, natural gas, and oil). CO_2 is a naturally occurring gas in the environment. It is used by plants to produce oxygen. Unfortunately, human combustion of fossil fuels (e.g.

automobiles, trucks, factories, etc.) since industrialization exceeds the amount that plants around the world can actually absorb. The leftover CO_2 which can't be absorbed by plants becomes a greenhouse gas. According to the EPA (US Environmental Protection Agency), CO_2 comprises approximately 82% of all greenhouse gases. Another 10% of greenhouse gases are comprised of methane gas which is emitted during the production and transport of coal, natural gas, and oil, as well as, livestock. Both nitrous oxide and fluorocarbons contribute the remaining 8% of greenhouse gases.

Global warming and the greenhouse effect caused by human activity (largely the combustion of fossil fuels) is an undeniable scientific fact; regardless of what the bizarre nonsensical conspiracy theorists say. The argument that reducing greenhouse gas emissions will somehow translate to lost jobs is also meritless and political grandstanding. Unless you happen to have another Earth in your back pocket, it behooves all of us to take care of the only earth we currently have. We only have two options available to us to truly address reducing greenhouse gas effect either a) reduce greenhouse gas emissions or b) significantly increase plants & vegetation.

The more direct option is to reduce greenhouse gas emissions. While I applaud the nearly (200) countries across the world that recognize climate change is a pressing issue for humanity and approved the Paris Climate Accord, I think this is only a first very important step. The United States should not only immediately approve and endorse the Paris Climate Agreement, but we should take further steps to reduce our greenhouse gas emissions well beyond the requirements of this accord. America has the technology and know-how to lead the world in both reducing greenhouse gases and the combustion of fossil fuels. So, why aren't we doing that today?

Well, we have several major industries and corporations in the United States that have historically thwarted the efforts to diversify America away from a fossil fuel based economy. Notably both auto manufacturers (e.g. Ford, GM, Honda, etc.) and petroleum producers (e.g. Exxon, BP, Shell, etc.) have economic vested interest in maintaining our dependency on oil. These corporations by themselves do not represent the best interest of the United States or our citizens. Frankly, from a US geo-political strategic perspective, eliminating our dependency on any and all oil based products greatly improves our strength and independence as a nation. Now, don't expect any of the suits from the c-suite of Exxon or BP to fess up to that fact, but it's true.

Environment

Americans have always risen to meet great challenges whether it was surviving the Great Depression, winning multiple world wars, or placing a man on the moon. America is greatest when we are challenged with rightful and noble causes. Eliminating our dependency on oil, while simultaneously reducing greenhouse gases impact on global climate change is just such a rightful and noble cause for America!

To this end, I would like to challenge congress to pass legislation which would ensure by the year 2028 that ALL new cars sold in the United States will not be petroleum or fossil combustion based. We have the technologies today to make this a reality in the United States, especially within the next decade. We simply need the political will and desire to make it happen.

Also, any company/corporation that is "squatting" on energy technology patents merely to keep the technology off the market should be pursued. Under the tenants of Eminent Domain, such patents should be seized and released to the public domain. If Eminent Domain permits the seizure of an individual citizen's property to construct a freeway, because it is in the public's best interest and welfare; the government certainly has the right to seize alternative fuel patents that companies like Exxon, BP, or GM, etc. may be squatting on.

Robert Marks

Federal Income Taxes

Next to death there aren't many topics more feared than the Federal Income Taxes. Frankly, I know a lot of folks who are more comfortable talking about death. It may surprise folks but for a large history of the United States we had no federal income tax, whatsoever. With the exception of briefly imposing an income tax during the Civil War and then again during the panic of the 1890s, the United States did not impose a permanent federal income tax until 1913. It wasn't until February 3, 1913 that the 16th amendment was adopted which established:

> *"The Congress shall have power to lay and collect taxes on incomes, from whatever source derived, without apportionment among the several states, and without regard to any census or enumeration.*

Federal Income Tax

Since 1913, income taxes have been a way of life. This is largely how the US government pays for federal programs, whether military, Social Security, education, Medicare, Transportation or any other federal program. As with most things in the United States, at first federal income tax was a pretty straightforward, simple idea. The tax forms were even short and straight forward too. Folks would simply pay a portion of the income they earned to help fund the federal government, which benefits us all.

It didn't take long before the politicians crawled out from beneath their rocks to co-opt this simple principle of federal income tax. Depending on their political agenda at the time, politicians would either strive to increase or decrease taxes altogether, add deductions which were tax-exempt, provide temporary tax relief in the form of tax credits, or even codify little-known loopholes for their buddies at the country club.

Unfortunately, the result of 100 years of political tinkering and unbridled gamesmanship has created a needlessly complex, intricate, and confounding federal tax code. This has spawned an industry into its own, filled to the brim with tax preparers, advisors, and lawyers. Not to mention an army of IRS agents to validate the legitimacy of tax filings. Oh yes, less we forget the proctology exam worthy IRS Audit. If you are wealthy enough today, you can hire a team of lawyers and accountants to find every tax credit, deduction, and available loophole there is in the federal tax code; while largely avoiding your tax responsibilities. Thus giving rise to the popular maxim, "Only suckers pay taxes."

If you didn't pick up on the nuanced use of the term "suckers", they are referencing you and me, pal. Personally, I hate being called a sucker. Frankly, I'm a little tired that the tax code has been so overwrought and contrived, that only a lawyer and CPA can tackle it, while their wealthy clients avoid paying taxes altogether. Are regular folks leaving money on the table because they can't afford a high-priced expert tax team? You and I both know the answer is a resounding "yes". Taxes are a fun little game for the rich, but let's face it the cards are stacked against the common man on this one.

Unless you are some kind of twisted masochist who enjoys inflicting pain on yourself, filing taxes is a complete and utter beat down. We desperately need to simplify our tax code to ensure that everyone is paying their fair share with no fancy hidden loopholes, deductions, or credits for the rich. Filing taxes annually should not be a time-consuming, ulcer inducing, all weekend affair every year. Ideally, filing income taxes should take no more than 10 minutes.

Federal Income Tax

Taxes needn't be so complicated and they can be significantly simplified. Additionally, we need to ensure that we have a progressive tax model in place to make certain everyone is paying their fair share. Those individuals with lower incomes should not be unduly burdened. We should implement a stratified flat rate income tax based on annual income, while eliminating ALL tax deductions, credits, and loopholes from our tax code with the exception of the Dependents deduction on Personal Taxes, as larger families do consume more household resources. All other deductions, credits, and loopholes should be quickly discontinued, especially for the rich and especially for corporations.

The following table of tax rates would increase overall tax revenues by eliminating the complex tax breaks given to both corporations & the wealthy, while simplifying the overall process (see *Proposed Tax Rate* table next page). By implementing this tax model, eliminating deductions, credits, and loopholes, and greatly simplifying the process we should increase our net tax revenues by $450 Billion annually. I would like to see the GAO/CBO independently run the numbers to confirm and validate the expectations of this model.

Proposed Tax Rate Table

Annual Income	Flat Tax Rate
Personal Federal Income Tax Rate	
$0 - $50 k	2%
$50 – 75 k	7%
$75 – $250 k	12%
$250 – $500 k	17%
$500 – $1,000 k	23%
$1,000 k – over	29%
Corporate Federal Income Tax Rate	
$0 - $1,000 k	17%
$1,000 k - over	23%
Long- Term Capital Gains Tax Rate	
$0 - $1,000 k	17%
$1,000 k – over	23%
Estate Taxes	
$0 - $1,000 k	5%
$1,000 k – over	23%

Fly the Belligerent Skies

Officially, irrefutably, categorically and without a doubt, Airlines suck. The folks at J.D. Powers, who just awarded the industry with the "Highest Customer Service Satisfaction Rating" in history (according to the J.D. Power 2017 North America Airline Satisfaction Study[SM]) need to pull their heads out of their backsides. For the record, nobody from J.D. Powers called me for my view about airlines. Had they, we would still be on the phone and their ears would be bleeding.

Before I ever consider flying the "Belligerent Skies" as an option for any of my travel needs, I first apply a ten hour pain threshold. What the heck is that? It's my own standard of what I am willing to drive before remotely considering air travel. If I can drive anywhere in ten hours or less from a time perspective it's usually a push compared to the time it would take to fly to the same destination and more importantly I get less ulcers. The ten hours it takes to drive my car translates to about a (600) mile radius from my home.

As everyone knows, there is a lot of wasted time in flying. Depending on where you live, it may take anywhere from 30 minutes to one hour just to drive to the airport. It will take 20-30 minutes to park your car, grab all your goodies, and schlepp to the ticket counter, where undoubtedly a long queue already awaits for your enjoyment. Once you are through the ticket counter queue, you will need to allow another 2 ½ hours for your scheduled orifice exam. We humans don't really have that many orifices; you would think the bright folks at TSA could speed the exams up. Nonetheless, 2 ½ hours is pushing the window. At some airports (e.g. O'Hare for example.), it may actually take 3 hours plus to navigate the security gauntlet.

So you have made it past Check Point Charlie. Now it's time for you to hustle to the gate, where hopefully your plane has not been delayed by weather, air traffic, mechanical, or pilot strike (thank you very little, Spirit Airline). Good news, there are no delays for your flight. Let the boarding cattle call begin. Now cross your fingers that your airline hasn't oversold the flight or some other yahoo pilot doesn't need to get to Kansas City; in either situation you may not be flying today at all.

Fly the Belligerent Skies

More good news, yes the airline oversold their plane and yes another pilot needed to get to Kansas City; however the "gods of flight" have smiled upon you today and bounced another poor unsuspecting family from the flight. Of course there's the predictable delay as the flight crew confronts the chosen family to inform them that they have been selected to scrap their vacation plans and not fly today. More delay as the police are called for the obligatory scuffle resulting from the escalated confrontation initiated by the airline crew. The cops take extra time and care to rub the father's face good and hard into the aisle carpet. Still more delay waiting for medics to arrive and patch the bleeding head wounds of the now beaten father. You get the picture?

Okay the poor schmuck and his family are now safely off the airplane, cooling their heels in the local jail. Ignore the fact that they did nothing wrong. Finally time to fly the belligerent skies, woohoo! We are now on the downhill drag. We want to get to grandma's house, so we start our journey from Cincinnati with the goal of flying to Kansas City; pretty simple goal huh? For some inexplicable reason the airline flies due east for two hours to Washington Dulles Airport, where you will catch your connector to Kansas City. Once you finally land at Dulles you taxi to the gate, grab all your goodies, de-board the plane and haul ass like a crazy person in a 70's Hertz commercial running across the airport in the hopeful pursuit of your connecting gate. Again hope to goodness your connecting plane is not overbooked and you don't get bumped by the airline. If the weather is clear and the creeks don't rise, your connecting flight lifts off only to retrace the original air flight to Cincinnati before continuing to Kansas City for your final destination.

Hopefully, you didn't check any bags. Please say you didn't. Grab all your goodies wait for the car rental shuttle which only runs every 15 to 20 min and head to the car rental counter. Undoubtedly, you will find yet another queue, standing behind someone with an expired Groupon, pitching a hissy fit. Check out of the car rental, sign your third child away, pick up your car, and finally you are on your way to grandma's house.

Personally I would rather undergo a painful root canal then have to fly anywhere. That is why I have established my ten hour threshold of pain for driving instead of flying. Unfortunately, if you have to fly somewhere there's not a lot of choices you have; only a handful of airlines still exist after the merger craze and all of them pretty much stink. Southwest Airlines use to be tolerable thirty years ago; however they have since adopted the "Delta-esque" customer service model. In over thirty-five years of flying, I have only found one single domestic airline, which doesn't make me vomit. This one single bright spot in an otherwise dismal industry is Ultimate Air, a small regional private charter airline out of Cincinnati. Unfortunately, they only fly to handful of cities, the prices are comparable to big airlines, and they do fly direct with no connections.

Again for the record I have no affiliation or interest in Ultimate Air whatsoever. I have no ownership and don't even know anyone who works there. Personally, I like Ultimate Air's business model and hope that other small airlines may follow suit to give travelers viable flight options. Ultimate Air operates smaller jet planes, which are well appointed with leather seats and additional legroom. In addition they fly to smaller regional airports, which greatly reduce the time it takes to get in and out of the airport. Lastly they actually have this strange concept known as "good customer service". They provide a very comfortable private lounge, complete with breakfast Danish and coffee. The pilots and stewardesses hand load your luggage onto the plane and personally greet you as you board. Once you are airborne, they serve a complementary alcoholic beverage of your choice if you desire. You receive all of this for about the same price that Delta charges to abuse and assault you. Literally, there is no comparison whatsoever to a Delta experience.

My hope is that our capitalist free market competition will ultimately solve the epidemic service problems of Airlines today. Delta is just a symptom of a much wider epidemic. Unequivocally, there is an endless customer demand, for better airline services in the United States. A smart entrepreneur could easily capitalize on the laughable customer service of large airlines with a smaller service focused airline flying directly to regional airports. Much like Ultimate Air does today.

Unfortunately the large airlines have a virtual stranglehold on available gates at international airports and unfairly block smaller competitors from their protected turf. It will certainly take a long time for the organic growth of smaller airlines to take hold and supplant the industry behemoths. In the meantime, I believe it is incumbent on our Congress to add additional airline regulations focused on protecting the consumer and preventing the continued exploitation by the greedy airline executives. And please don't talk to me about the current and pathetic Airline Passenger Bill of Rights. We need protective legislation with real teeth.

A few consumer protective regulations that should be considered by Congress and enacted would greatly reduce the frustration and hostilities prevailing in the airline industry today. I believe it should be illegal for an airline to oversell a flight. It seems common sense to me that you can't sell something you ain't got. If the airline only has (200) seats for a given flight than that should be all that the Airline is legally allowed to sell. Not (210) while hoping that ten people don't show up, but only selling what they actually have available. I believe overselling flights is simply fraud and should be prosecuted. Again the airline is selling something they simply don't have. I certainly don't know a clearer definition of fraud.

Another area we could focus on is establishing minimum mandatory legroom of (36) inches for every seat on the plane. I understand that the airline can squeeze more profits out of a single flight if they reduced legroom and pack the passengers in like sardines. Heck if they could figure out how to do it, I am certain that they would prefer consumers to physically stand during a flight. A rather ridiculous, far-fetched thought, but don't put it past the greed of the airlines to pursue this. There are airline industry proposals today that the already tight legroom should be reduced to an unbearable (29) inches per seat. Meaning you couldn't lean back in your seat without banging the knees of the passenger in the row behind you. The additional legroom would greatly reduce the occurrence of in-flight conflict erupting between passengers, which are actually quite dangerous to everyone on board.

Lastly, I would like to focus consumer protection measures on financial remuneration and remedy for airlines that failed to live up to their end of the bargain. Consumers have already paid large sums of money to book the flight in the first place and should have a contractual expectation that the airline lives up to their end of the deal. The airline certainly accepted payment from the passengers in advance and have committed to providing a certain level of service in consideration of the payment, I believe that they should be financially held to delivering on that commitment.

We need to determine a reasonable amount (but more punitive than provided by the Passenger Bill of rights) that airlines should pay passengers for any deviation whatsoever in the Airlines execution of the specified flight. I do not care what caused the schedule deviation, whether it was man-made or an act of God. Bottom line the airline has not delivered their commitment, and should be punished accordingly. We could establish a reasonable time window of say one hour delay of flight schedule before penalties would be assessed. But once that hour is exceeded, I believe it's the airlines responsibility to fairly compensate the passengers for the delay and their time. I would suggest for simple flight delays, the hourly salary rate of the highest paid executive at the Airline multiplied by the time delay would be reasonable for each passenger to receive. Time is money and your time is no less valuable than the CEO of the Airline. If flights are canceled altogether again, regardless of reason, I believe the airline should be penalized full cost reimbursement to the passenger plus preset set punitive treble damages. All assessed penalties would be immediately payable and due in cash, not bullshit airline vouchers or a check.

In addition to preventing airlines from selling something they don't have, specifically overselling seats, airlines should be blocked from bumping a previously paid passenger from the flight, simply to use their seat for any of their own employees, employees' families, acquaintances, or anyone else they like better. I understand that airlines may have a need to periodically move pilots and flight teams from one airport to another for business purposes. However, this is the airline's logistical issue to deal with and resolve, not the passengers issue to deal with and resolve. No passenger should ever be affected or remotely inconvenienced due to an airline's logistical, operational, personnel, or scheduling inefficiencies and incompetency.

Robert Marks

Freedom of Speech

One of our greatest blessings in this country is our Freedom of Speech. Even so, of all of our rights this is the one that creates the most difficulty and angst for me to balance. I am certainly not a fan of extremist on either side. When I hear these nut jobs spewing their venomous hatred against everyday ordinary Americans, it is so very difficult for me to turn the other cheek and recognize that in our great country even these idiots have a right to voice their beliefs. But they DO have the right, after all they are Americans. Even if I personally find their hatred laced vomit reprehensible, this does not discount or diminish their right to say what is on their mind.

In April of this year, the kids at Berkeley hopefully learned a lifelong lesson regarding freedom of speech. An ultra-right wing nut was scheduled to come on campus and spew her hatred. Understandably the students at Berkeley recoiled at the prospect of this possibility. Soon threats of violence, protests, and demonstrations ran rampant across the university campus, the Berkeley community, and the tweeto-sphere. While, I understand the student's feelings and disgust with the speaker in question, this was a wrong approach. First off, violence or the threat of violence is never the answer. If anything, this actually helps to support, legitimize, and justify the extremist views; making them appear more reasonable then they actually are. And the student's fear that just because some nut says outrageous comments, somehow these comments will magically become reality is simply ungrounded. These types of inflammatory extremist views cater to a small fringe minority.

From an individual basis I support our citizen's right to freedom of speech, even though I often find myself holding my nose at what is being said. It is our very freedom of speech that is expressly allowing me to write down my thoughts today, while recognizing that some folks may not like what I say and might even take offense to it. Even though I support freedom of speech, it literally galls the living hell out of me to watch an American citizen deface or burn the American flag. Specifically in light of the millions of men and women over the centuries that have given their blood for this freedom of speech, I believe any defacing of the American flag is a callous, cowardly, and insensitive act. Nonetheless, I would be among the first to defend these individuals, the opportunity to express their thoughts and this most sacred right of freedom of speech. Even while defending their right to speech, I would be deeply conflicted by what they had done. Thank goodness our forefathers were much wiser and insightful than me.

Perhaps one of the most important areas of freedom of speech in our democracy is that of our media and news outlets. Both of these serve as an important check and balance to our leaders in this democracy. Throughout history totalitarian regimes have routinely blocked, prohibited, intimidated, or censored news outlets. The Nazis did this in Germany, Saddam Hussein in Iraq, Kim Jong-Un in North Korea; history is replete with the repression of independent news media. The problem is without the free and unfettered access of the news media, the public is fed a steady diet of state sponsored propaganda; truth goes out the window and the citizens are victimized. In recent months some US politicians have painted the news media and news outlets, as enemies of the state. I don't know what state they're referencing, but this is certainly a dangerous and slippery slope. Some politicians have gone as far as suggesting that news outlets and their sources should not be protected by freedom of speech. Again this is a frightening prospect, which I would expect in a totalitarian regime not the United States.

Freedom of Speech

Personally I prefer to get my news and information from a multitude of different sources. Whether it's ABC, CBS, NBC, BBC, CNN, MSNBC, POST, NY TIMES, or even late-night satire by various comedians; I like to formulate my opinions after hearing from many credible sources. I can't imagine limiting my information to a single source for news or world events, specifically if that source is pushing continual propaganda for a specific political agenda without consideration to either truth or impartiality. The folks lapping up the propaganda infused cherry Kool-Aid from Al Jazeera or Fox News 24 x 7, should expand their horizons. Frankly, I find Fox News to be the less credible of the two. While I'll never bother tuning in to these apparent propaganda networks, I will defend their and every News outlet's right to report the news as they see fit, maintain the confidentiality of sources, and protect their freedom of speech.

While I believe that both American citizens and their news outlets have to be protected by a robust freedom of speech, I do not believe that this freedom necessarily extends to known terrorist organizations in America. As I mentioned before I'm somewhat conflicted regarding freedom of speech and believe reasonable safeguard measures need to be applied to this basic freedom. For example, I believe it is wrong to scream "fire" in a movie theater or "bomb" in a crowded airport. Regardless that freedom of speech is a guarantee for our citizens, this type of recklessness would ensue riots and panic. Another area that I believe it is prudent to limit freedom of speech is by known terrorist organizations. While I agree that citizens should have the right and the freedom to speak their mind, regardless if it is widely accepted, I do not believe that a person should be allowed to speak their mind while representing or promoting a known terrorist organization in America.

This means a citizen would have the right to spew their hatred publically, but NOT while wearing a soiled bedsheet and white hood, as this would represent a known terrorist organization. This would extend to any known terrorist organization, which seeks to undermine America whether it's the KKK, neo-Nazis, Al Qaeda, ISIS or other such groups. Known terrorist organizations should not be permitted to use our very freedoms against us as a means to recruit new members. I believe a very solid review and appeal process would need to be developed and implemented before designating a group, as a known terrorist organization. But once that is done, the group would no longer be protected by freedom of speech.

Gerrymandering

Beyond the farce that is our Electoral College, another issue we desperately need to fix in our Democracy is the practice of gerrymandering. For those who are not familiar with this favored dirty-little, nefarious, trick; gerrymandering is little more than stacking the cards in your electoral favor. Whichever party is in power, they have the authority to redraw electoral districts, however they see fit. And boy, do they!

This was granted originally for very logical and real reasons. Specifically, we need to ensure and have a mechanism to redraw electoral districts to map back with population growth and decline. This is a perfectly reasonable reason to redraw electoral districts. While there is a real need to occasionally redraw electoral districts, our wonderful politicians have used this device to both gain power and deny power to others. How do they do this? Simply with a stroke of the pen, they can draw outlandish districts on either the basis of race, religion, or party affiliation. Technically drawing the districts on the basis of race or religion is not permitted, but only a fool would think that our politicians aren't exploiting this to their own benefit under the guise of "party affiliation". That is how you get famous gerrymandered districts like the "salamander district", the "earmuffs district", or any other contrived and crafted district. Given the latitude that the party in power has to redraw districts, successful court challenges are few and far between. What this means at the end of the day is some folks are under-represented while other folks are over-represented.

We cannot get rid of the need to periodically redraw electoral maps to rebalance for population shifts this is a reality. However, we can put an end to the freehand drawing of favorable political districts for self gain. As I mentioned earlier, I believe in one man, one woman, one vote. The majority wins and we should not artificially deny the will of the people, which we routinely do today through gerrymandering.

Perhaps the best way to ensure that political districts are not favorably drawn to benefit any single party, race, or religion is to ensure that all districts are drawn using the geometric shape of a square. Next, all districts would have to be balanced from a population perspective. This will allow districts to be enlarged or shrunk to map to the population. In states that have unique boundaries, the geometric shape of a square could extend beyond their boundaries such that the portion of the geometric shape within the state is balanced from a population perspective to all other districts within the state. No more fun and games for the party bosses in the smoke-filled back rooms of America. Sorry boys the jig is up.

Removing the practice of gerrymandering would affect a sea change in our political landscape in America. This would return the power to the citizens and remove the power from self-serving politicians. While I fervently believe that we must outlaw gerrymandering in the United States, the fact of the matter is it likely will never go away. This is simply because the folks, who are in power, want to stay in power. And these cowards are smart enough to recognize that they simply would not be in power anymore if political districts were redrawn without prejudice or preference. It is the very essence of prejudice and preference, which keeps them in power and receiving their cushy paycheck. Why on earth would they want to jeopardize this security? Show me a politician who says "gerrymandering doesn't exist" or "it's not a big problem" and I will show you an utterly corrupt politician.

GLBTA / LGBT

When I think of GLBTA and the associated rights, I am often reminded of the memorable lyrics of John Lennon:

"Whatever gets you through the night, it's all right, it's all right"

For all those other old fuddy-duddies like me that are out there, GLBTA (aka LGBT) stands for "Gay, Lesbian, Bisexual, Transgender, and Allies". I know this sounds naïve on my part, but I truly don't comprehend what the fuss is about GLBTA and why it simply is not an accepted fact of life. Folks are born the way they are born. Get over it!

Specifically, I don't understand why disinterested individuals care one way or the other if two consenting adults are in a loving relationship; regardless of the specifics of that relationship. As a heterosexual, I could care less if another man prefers blondes over brunettes. Likewise, why would it bother me if a woman is attracted to tall men? Or if a married couple is inter-racial or inter-faith. To me all of this is nothing more than personal preference and falls under the heading of individual rights. So too, I don't particularly have an opinion if a man is attracted to another man, a woman to another woman, if they are attracted to both sexes, or if some folks ain't comfortable in their own skin and wanna fix it. None of these situations affect me or my family one iota. I simply do not understand why some folks have such a profound issue against empowering others to live their life as they choose in pursuit of their individual happiness. Get your noise out of other people's business!

I know, I know, I know; I have heard the Old Testament argument (Leviticus 18:22) before. But this ain't Bible school and oh by the way, here in the United States we observe a little notion called separation of church and state. I would ask all you self-righteous Bible thumper's, who live and die by Leviticus, to give it a rest when we're discussing human rights in the United States of America. I understand it may be hard to comprehend but not everyone in America has the same religious beliefs that you may have. Remember the 1st Amendment? It's ok here in America if folks hold and practice different religious beliefs from our own. Leviticus 18:22 is not the end all be all of life in

America, nor should it be. Personally, I'm a practicing Christian. Nonetheless, our personal religious views should not be used as the sole basis for what human rights are granted in our society. But given our separation of church state, I believe we have to respect individual's choices and protect everyone's human rights without overlaying our personal religious beliefs.

Now there are real implications in our society that we have to ensure everyone has equal access to. Whether its marriage licenses, insurance coverage, beneficiaries, living will, adoption, or any other situation in life with legal implications; we need to ensure everyone is treated fairly and equally. As a compassionate society, we need to treat everyone with dignity and respect regardless of sexual orientation or preference. Likewise, we need to ensure these legal proceedings are administered without prejudice. The Kentucky clerk who refused to perform her duties and issue Marriage Licenses based on sexual orientation should have been horse whipped!

One of the dumbest conflicts around GLBTA rights that I've heard of recently is the bathroom brawl over Transgender restrooms in North Carolina. Really? We care what bathroom somebody uses to relieve themselves. I am 53 years old and have seen my fair share of Jimmy Buffett, Willie Nelson, ZZ Top, and numerous other concerts. One thing that is consistent in these concerts is that the guy's restroom line is very short while the girl's line stretches for eternity. I never knew if it was the difference in male or female plumbing or what actually caused this phenomenon. Nonetheless, I assure you every concert or sporting event that I have ever attended regardless of genre had a similar restroom situation. Given this reality, I cannot count how many times I have witnessed women who were fed up with standing in the endless girl's line jump over to the guy's shorter line to do their business. It never bothered anyone when this happened. Why is it bothering folks now in North Carolina? Do the good folks in North Carolina use the potty differently than everyone else in America?

I really do not know why folks would be all worked up over which bathroom a person chooses to use. When nature calls, nature calls. Regarding North Carolina, I do applaud the numerous artists, companies, and sporting venues that have opted to avoid North Carolina until they reluctantly join the 21st century. I also applaud the folks who stand up for these human dignities across America, each and every day. Personally, I am very proud to call myself an "ally" of the LGBT movement.

Robert Marks

Gun Control

Well I'm apt to upset everyone with this topic. The water is fine, so let's dive straight in. I am both a supporter of robust gun control and the 2nd Amendment. Bizarre, huh? Before you get out the tar and feathers let me explain myself and reconcile the differences. The 2nd Amendment provides:

> *"A well-regulated Militia, being necessary to the security of a Free State, the right of the people to keep and bear Arms, shall not be infringed."*

Nonetheless, I believe this right must be controlled with reasonable safeguards to protect society. Unfortunately, the Second Amendment doesn't expressly define what constitutes "Arms". Even so, I am reasonably sure that most rational Americans, do not believe that the Second Amendment empowers citizens to bear a nuclear weapon for example. And yet a nuclear weapon is a weapon employed by armies and militaries. In other words a nuclear weapon is in fact, "Arms".

Clearly the Second Amendment was not designed to suggest that citizens could bear any military grade weapons, but rather that they could defend themselves by bearing arms. To me this would extend to pistols, rifles, shotguns, knives, axes, and hatchets. All of these can legitimately be used by citizens to protect their homes, defend their families, or provide food through hunting. I do not believe that the 2nd Amendment extends to military grade weapons such as machine guns, automatic pistols, assault rifles, chemical/biological bombs, nuclear weapons, or other weapons of mass destruction.

In addition to controlling what types of weapons are permitted by the 2nd Amendment, it is a prudent safeguard for Society to ensure reasonable background and psychological checks are performed on any citizen acquiring or possessing a firearm. These checks should be universal without consideration of how the firearm was acquired inclusive of internet, trade shows, pawn shops, gun shows, private sales, bartering, inheritance, lost and found, pre-manufactured gun kits requiring assembly, or even self-manufactured guns. In addition to background checks, we should implement a National minimum age of eighteen before a firearm can be purchased or even possessed. No one under this age should be permitted to purchase, acquire, or possess a firearm at all.

With the exception of private homes, private properties, farms, and/or hunting leases; the government (Federal, State and local Municipalities) should be empowered to regulate where bearing a firearm is permitted. Several places come to mind and should be prohibited from citizens bearing guns within: governmental offices, courts, schools, day cares, hospitals, places of worship, sporting events, airports, seaports, bus/train stations, or any public venues where more than two people are gathered. I am quite sure there are many, many more places to add to this list where guns should not be permitted, but you get the point. Guns and people simply don't mix. None of these places should ever have a gun remotely near it, unless carried by authorized law enforcement. And stop your whining about your "right to bear arms"; I am getting to that.

Now let's address the elephant in the room, the 2nd Amendment. The pro-gun folks will argue from the rafters that this Amendment provides the right to bear arms and I agree; it does. Feel better? I agreed with ya. However, I would argue that these pro-gun folks are conveniently glossing over the first part of the amendment, which is the most important part. Perhaps, the first part of the amendment doesn't serve their purposes or end goals, so they conveniently ignore it. But I don't ignore it, nor should anyone else. The 2nd Amendment actually provides for a "well-regulated" militia. This is in fact why the Amendment exists in the first place. Maintaining a well-regulated Militia is the ONLY reason that the right to bear arms is guaranteed at all, specifically the beginning phrase:

> *"A well-regulated Militia, being necessary to the security of a Free State..."*

I agree, the 2nd Amendment guarantees the right to bear arms in order to maintain a "well-regulated militia", which could be called upon in times of national need. However, America's need to maintain a well-regulated militia doesn't mean every John Wayne wanna-be gets to run around with his new shiny pop-pistol. The expectation of our founding fathers, clearly states that we should "well-regulate" this militia. Regulating the types of permissible firearms, the necessary background and psychological screening, minimum age, and establishing the places those firearms are/are not permitted fulfills the essence of a well-regulated militia. Please do not preach to me about your precious 2nd Amendment rights without reading the **ENTIRE** amendment, which incidentally I support.

Robert Marks

HealthCare

Every person on United States soil regardless of race, religion, sex, or orientation has the right and expectation to qualified HealthCare. Not healthcare if you can afford it, have a job, or don't have any pre-existing conditions, but rather HealthCare for everyone regardless of your personal situation. It is our society's obligation to lift up and protect those less fortunate than ourselves. In doing so, it is our government's responsibility to provide Universal HeathCare for every soul in America, just as they provide military to protect our shores, education to advance our knowledge, libraries for our reference, parks for our enjoyment, and roads to traverse.

This is easier said than done. Obamacare was a heroic effort to provide universal care. However, the program was fatally flawed from the beginning as it failed to address the fundamental issues at hand with HealthCare, specifically medical cost. Obamacare sought to leverage the existing mechanisms and institutions in our HealthCare industry, while extending health coverage to all individuals. The theory was that more individuals who were covered would help drive down the costs for all. The problem with that model was it discounted the ongoing profiteering by medical providers, who were simply not incented to reduce their costs. There are several fundamental problems with our HealthCare system today that have to be scrapped and overhauled if we are to provide cost affordable universal HealthCare for everyone.

The first issue that has to be addressed is the concept of free-market capitalism in HealthCare. I am a huge free-market capitalist by nature, however, capitalism simply does not work in HealthCare. We need to accept this fact and modify our healthcare accordingly. The reason is very simple in a free-market capitalist model; we need two parties to participate in a financial transaction, buyer and seller. The buyer and seller reach a mutually beneficial negotiated price and a transaction occurs. If the buyer and seller can't reach a negotiated price, then the buyer can shop other options.

This is pure capitalism at its essence, which is very successful in most situations, but not healthcare. There can be no undue influence on either buyer or seller in a pure capitalist model, as this would constitute extortion not capitalism. To illustrate the difference between capitalism and extortion, picture a Mafiosi selling "protection insurance" to a small shop owner. "Buy our insurance and your building won't mysteriously burn down." Even though a product is being sold and there is both a buyer and a seller, this is an example of extortion not capitalism. The shop owner in this scenario doesn't really have a choice to fairly negotiate given the situation or even a realistic option to shop for other options.

The reason that capitalism doesn't work in HealthCare is very similar. The buyer, also known as the patient, has undue extortive pressure and influence placed on them. The undue pressure that prevents them from engaging in a fair negotiation on their behalf is their very health or the health of their loved ones. As a result the patient is not in a position to freely negotiate the price that they are willing to pay for a medical product/service or shop for other options. Accordingly the free market capitalist model is instantly broken and fails. As a result patients are often held hostage by medical providers, labs, hospitals, and of course pharmaceuticals while enduring enormous extortive pressures.

Does anyone really believe that an unconscious accident victim, wheeled into an emergency room for life-saving treatment is in a position to negotiate a fair and reasonable price for the services they receive or shop for other options, of course not? Does anyone else believe that a parent whose child has life-threatening allergies is in the position to negotiate the price of say an Epi-Pen? These are just two examples, obviously there are countless more examples of price gauging, extorting, and profiteering by medical providers. So how do we fix this mess?

Healthcare is an extremely complex problem given the numerous parties and competing interest that are involved. In the current environment doctors, hospitals, labs, lawyers, pharmaceuticals, and insurance companies are all vying for profits largely at the expense of the patient. This is why medical costs are so astronomically high; everyone wants to get a piece of the pie. The patient, however, is not motivated by profit but rather by their health. In order to solve this problem and provide affordable universal HealthCare, we need to level set the playing field and dramatically reduce costs across the board.

We should immediately simplify the HealthCare equation and remove or eliminate non-contributing players from the conversation. Obviously patients pursuing health and welfare will always be the driving force in HealthCare and should be. Likewise, critical players in the health equation are the medical providers, labs, hospitals, device providers, and pharmaceuticals that provide health services and products for patients.

Did anyone catch the two groups that I did not mention? These groups do not provide the patient's demand for health services nor do they provide any of the medical services and products that patients require. These groups literally provide no HealthCare value in the equation whatsoever. Instead these groups are solely interested in producing profits for their shareholders, while costing patients and the system a lot of money. These needless "middle-men" are easy groups to remove from HealthCare, which will help to reduce overall medical cost. I'm speaking about the health-insurance industry and lawyers, both are parasitic leeches in HealthCare providing no medical services or value. Neither has ever cured anything.

By removing these groups out of the health equation, we solve many of the problems that plague our current HealthCare environment. Without Insurance companies in the mix, the concept of pre-existing condition goes away. The idea of limiting choice of health providers by designating "in network" or "out of network" is also eliminated. Denial of services or claims is no longer applicable. The marketing scam of medical plans and deductibles also vanishes. And employers are no longer involved in providing or paying for employee health insurance. By removing lawyers from the equation, we reduce the threat of millions in malpractice and the enormous cost associated with malpractice insurance. This one stroke of eliminating both health insurance companies and lawyers from the HealthCare conversation greatly reduces the contrived complexities of providing universal HealthCare, as well as, the inherent cost. This must be the first step taken.

Now with a simpler HealthCare equation, we are left with only true medical providers and patients in the Health equation. But as we discussed earlier the patients are not in a position to negotiate reasonable prices to pay for medical products or services. This was supposed to be the services that insurance companies could provide at negotiating prices on behalf of the patients. However, the Insurance Company's first master is their shareholders and profits not the patients. Accordingly, it is far too easy for health insurance companies to exploit, impede, block, and limit patient's care for their own selfish profits and self-interest with contrived barriers. This is done routinely thru various nefarious techniques like pre-existing conditions, denial of claim, permitted network, or countless other techniques.

As patients are not in a position to negotiate HealthCare prices and Insurance companies are fundamentally conflicted, we need a truly independent and dis-interested third-party to unilaterally negotiate, set, and affect those acceptable prices across the HealthCare industry. We should establish a new governmental HealthCare agency expressly chartered with responsibility of negotiating and setting acceptable prices across the HealthCare industry; everything from a simple tongue depressor used in an office visit to an intricately complex heart transplant, all the necessary pharmaceuticals, and any required medical devices; everything soup to nuts.

By empowering one single group with responsibility to set universal prices, we can eliminate the price gouging and profiteering currently embraced by our medical providers, device, and pharmaceutical companies. It is true, not all medical services are equal, some cost more to research, produce, and deliver. Most importantly, medical providers and pharmaceuticals should be properly incented to advance medical knowledge, skills, techniques, and care. This serves and benefits everyone. The universal pricing would need to be reasonably stratified in a manner to ensure more skilled and experienced physicians are appropriately compensated, as well as, pharmaceuticals with new life saving drugs. We should recognize this fact and stratifying prices accordingly. However, medical providers and pharmaceuticals should not be permitted to ruthlessly exploit patients for profiteering purposes by setting their own prices. All medical prices would have to be fairly and reasonably established and applied universally.

HealthCare

To make this work in America, any medical provider or pharmaceutical company that did not adhere to the established universal pricing for products and services would have their license removed from practicing in the United States. So if a pharmaceutical company decides to unilaterally and artificially inflate the price of one specific drug by 5,000% in violation of the established governmental price for the drug, then all of their pharmaceutical products would be banned from the US market. In addition to banning their products from our markets, the company would forfeit all related patents to the public domain. Ah, now we have level set the playing field and provided ample incentive to medical providers, device, and pharmaceutical companies to maintain reasonable pricing.

In this model fair and equitable prices are established for medical services and products by placing the medical providers in direct competition against one another. Providers who are unable to perform their services or products for the established universal price, would simply go out of business and be replaced by more efficient groups who could provide the services at the establish price. This will further drive industry efficiencies.

All HealthCare coverage would be universal. There would be no consideration of pre-existing condition prior to treatment, merely a referral by an attending physician. Everyone in the US would be covered for all necessary treatment. There would be no denial of services or pharmaceuticals if warranted and authorized by appropriate medical personnel. Coverage would extend to all legally claimed dependents. Also there would be no restriction on your choice of Physician or Heath Provider. And all medical associated bills by providers or pharmaceuticals would be paid directly by the government on a monthly basis with no out of pocket cost by the patient, other than $20 co-pay.

As we discussed earlier, HealthCare services and providers would be exempted from malpractice law-suits. I am personally not a huge fan of this last part, however, as a society we have to remove the threat of malpractice suits to reduce HealthCare cost for all of us. Also if HealthCare providers are no longer allowed to establish their own pricing but must adhere to universal pricing, this is a small and reasonable concession we should take. In lieu, of Malpractice Lawsuits, a review process would need to be implemented to consider potential cases. If the severity or frequency of the medical malpractice justifies, the penalty imposed would be probation up to full revocation of the license/right to practice medicine in the United States, but lawsuits would no longer be permitted.

So how do we pay for such a HealthCare system? I would propose that a reasonable approach would be a sliding scale charged per person based on their annual household income. For those individuals with household incomes (reported on Federal Income Taxes) up to $100,000 annually, they would pay $100 per month for each covered individual. This means a family of four would pay $400 a month if their annual income was less than $100,000. For families with household income up to $200,000, the cost would be set at $200 per month per covered person. The cost for coverage would increase by $100 per month for each $100,000 in annual household income with a cap established at $5 million in annual household income.

Individuals on welfare, who could not afford to pay out-of-pocket $100 per month, would have their monthly benefits reduced by the $100 cost. For any individuals who could not prove the filing of an annual Federal Income Tax statement and establish their annual household income, two social workers would independently evaluate the families living condition, estimate their annual income, and qualify them for HealthCare coverage. For these individuals who cannot prove the filing of federal income tax (which everyone should have), the cost would be double per month of the coverage rates previously discussed and applied to the estimated Annual Income estimates provided by the Social workers. Beyond the revenues raised by the assessment and collection of Monthly Premiums and co-pays for Universal Coverage, budget dollars previously allocated to Medicare, Medicaid, and VA Medical (see Military/Vets Section) would be distributed to the Universal Healthcare system. If we do this, we can ensure that all individuals in the United States would have access to affordable medical care.

Contrary to Obamacare, there would be no penalties or fines imposed for not paying for the Universal medical coverage. Services and medical products would simply be denied or withheld for those individuals who cannot prove Universal coverage in the US. This would be sufficient incentive to ensure all citizens actively seek coverage. Hospitals and providers would be authorized to turn away patients who did not have proof of universal coverage. We have to accept that this is true Universal Health Coverage for everyone, and no one would be exempted. If an individual chooses not to participate in the Universal Health Coverage program, then they have effectively chosen not to have HealthCare coverage in the United States.

One of the biggest costs we have today in HealthCare is that we routinely perform medical services (e.g. Emergency room visits, etc.) for individuals who cannot pay for the cost. These costs are transferred and absorbed by all others. Today, people without HealthCare coverage routinely use emergency rooms in lieu of going to a doctor's office for non-life threating illnesses to avoid out of pocket expense. Obviously this has to stop. You would have Universal HealthCare Coverage and be eligible for medical services under coverage or you would not have the required universal coverage and would have to pay 100% out of pocket. Universal means universal. Orphans, of course, would be provided coverage at no cost through the Universal HealthCare program.

By simultaneously simplifying the HealthCare equation, substantially reducing costs for medical services, devices, and pharmaceuticals across the industry, reallocating Medicaid, Medicare, VA Medical dollars, while increasing the pool of individuals who are actively participating and covered, we could provide Universal HealthCare in America.

The challenge that has to be met dictates that runaway medical costs must be reined in with an independent pricing established. Also we have to increase coverage participation to our entire population, which will afford more money to the HealthCare system as a whole. This is an important topic that will affect every person in America both directly and indirectly. HealthCare is a right and must be provided to all our citizens regardless of race, religion, sex, or orientation. I would like to see the GAO/CBO evaluate this proposal for both overage and cost. This is the AmeriCare Universal HealthCare approach.

Robert Marks

Human Rights

The topic of Human Rights truly is a difficult concept to get our heads wrapped around. It is abstract, nebulous, ever evolving, and viewed through different prisms of humanity's own existence. One person's human rights are another person's religious or social mores and vice versa. In 1948, an important document, the Universal Declaration of Human Rights, was adopted by the United Nations General Assembly.

The declaration was significant as it formally set forth the rights that all humans are guaranteed and should expect. Important to note, the declaration was written on the heel of two world wars and certainly does not include current considerations of sexual orientation. Nonetheless, many of the thirty Articles included are eloquent, noble, and quite moving. The Declaration is certainly an outstanding baseline definition of Human Rights that can be adapted to modernity.

Human Rights

Article I of the declaration largely sums up my personal perspective and aspirations regarding Human Rights:

> *"All human beings are born free and equal in dignity and rights. They are endowed with reason and conscience and should act towards one another in a spirit of brotherhood."*

If only the world would live up to those inspirational words. Many folks feel that the United States is the Human Rights capital of the world. Considering all the countries in the world, we do a fairly good job regarding Human Rights. But we are certainly not the world leader in this regard and most certainly have room for improvement, especially in the areas of Exploitation of Woman, LGBT Rights, Race, and Religion.

The objectification and commercialization of woman is pervasive in our society. It plays out on every beer, jean, or perfume commercial. It's plastered across the billboards of America's highways. And it is prominently displayed in our movies, television, magazines, and books. All of this is done under the adage that "sex sells". That may very well be true, but it likewise creates a dangerous situation that woman have to deal with every day and denies their human rights. Examples of these daily dangers for women are everywhere. This was recently displayed at one of the largest media news outlets in the country. Several well-known female news anchors were subjected to unwanted sexual advances and harassment by executive management under threat of being fired. Other examples of these dangers play out in frat houses on college campuses, underage sex, and date rapes. Sadly, we also see the impact of this in the sex trafficking of teenage girls and young women. As a society, we need to eliminate the objectification of woman and ensure all women's rights are protected.

In the LGBT (Lesbian, Gay, Bisexual, and Transgender) community, their human rights are also violated daily in America on the basis of their sexual orientation or preference. Whether its employers passing over promotions or even refusing to hire, small businesses refusing service, or even being ostracized in a community. The members of LGBT deal with these unjustified social barriers every day. More troubling is the violence directed at this community; everything from threats, to assault, murder, and even targeted terrorist assaults has been inflicted on LGBT members without discretion simply because of their sexual orientation. A painful example of this occurred in June 2016 when forty-nine people were killed and fifty-three more wounded at the Gay Nightclub, Pulse. This is horrific.

Human Rights

Regarding race, when as a society are we ever going to get past the race issues, mistrust, and hatred in America? It is incomprehensible in 2017 that crosses are still burning in communities across America. Whether it is in Louisiana, Idaho, or California; crosses are still being set ablaze to intimidate. Black churches across the south are also ablaze. Far too often these tactics of intimidation are taken further to violence. Such was the case in 2015, when nine people were killed and one wounded during bible study at a Charleston church. Innocent souls shot down during peaceful worship. As a result of the racial tensions today, police in many communities feel besieged and threatened. Likewise, minorities are afraid of being wrongly shot by the police. We must bring an end to this distrust. We are a diverse nation of immigrants, we need to embrace the worth and value of every single American, regardless of race.

On that note, we need to recognize and adhere to the importance of the 1st amendment. Specifically, that Americans have a right to worship as they see fit. If you truly believe in America, than you have to believe in this. Regardless if someone is Christian, Muslim, Jewish, Buddhist, Hindu, or any other faith, they have a right to worship in America without threat or violence. Not only do they have the right to worship, all people of every faith have the right to immigrate to America.

Robert Marks

Immigration

Really a wall?!? Why just a wall between the United States and Mexico? While we're at it, why not build a northern wall too between United States and Canada? Aren't we also afraid of the Canadians? Have you seen how freakin' polite they are? Canadians are absolutely relentless in their kindness. We simply can't let them into America! Possibly, a Canadian who may be less polite is that "Nasty Woman" Samantha Bee, who routinely emasculates day-old, stale, pompous, white bread politicians. However, the lying politicians really do deserve it! In good faith, we can't fault her for taking them to task.

Clearly Canadians have all been brain-washed to believe that women deserve equal pay, own their own uterus, can make up their own minds, and drive a car. What exactly would happen if they menstruated while driving? Oh my God, have you thought about that? We definitely need a (200) foot tall wall to keep all those polite, well-intentioned, nice Canadians out! Do

Immigration

we really want a country inundated with the likes of Celine Dion, Michael Bublé, Michael Fox, William Shatner, and Peter Jennings? No Canadians allowed!

A wall has to be the most asinine proposal. Am I the only person left that remembers the Berlin wall? Spoiler alert, it didn't exactly work out well for the USSR. Certainly as a country, we can and should protect our borders from drug traffickers or military incursions (the latter is highly unlikely). Electronic surveillance drones, and Border Patrol should suffice. However, a wall is just plum silly, ridiculously expensive, and diplomatically offensive to our Latin neighbors. A wall would be completely ineffective and would needlessly trample on thousands of property owners rights in the border states.

Full disclosure on this topic, I am actually a first generation American. You wouldn't know it by talking to me; I have a thick Texas accent, blonde (what ain't already gray) hair, blue eyes, and sound a bit like a bobcat in a blender. Still, I am a first generation American. My dad's family escaped Adolf Hitler and Nazi Germany in 1936 for the promise of a better life in America. His folks never learned to speak English. For lack of a better word, they were refugees. Papa went to college, was awarded the Purple Heart in the Korean War, got and stayed married, worked in the defense industry during the 'Missiles of

October', lovingly raised a family, paid taxes, and served as a Deacon in the local Presbyterian church. God Bless America and the American dream.

We are a country of immigrants, refugees, and dreamers just like my dad; a shining lantern of hope for the rest of the world. Best yet, this great melting pot of humanity has served us quite well as a country, through hundreds of years, a Great Depression, multiple world wars, even a trip to the moon; all in all not bad for a bunch of refugees and immigrants. Personally, I am no more afraid of a South American refugee or Syrian refugee than I would be of a Canadian. These are all humans, less we forget.

It does make sense to have a fair and efficient process in place to perform reasonable vetting to protect our current citizens. The emphasis here is a "fair" process, not based on some hysterical phobia, religious litmus test, educational level, artificial wealth test or any other stereotypical horse manure. The relentless political fear mongering and grand standing regarding immigration is simply meritless. No need to fear the immigrant boogey-man.

One of the challenges, which we as a compassionate nation must address, is providing a realistic and attainable path to citizenship. As I mentioned earlier on this topic, we are a nation of immigrants and dreamers. Remember, the Pilgrims had no immigration laws to contend with. While I agree we should not reward folks for breaking the law and immigrating illegally to the United States by blindly granted citizenship. Likewise it is not prudent to designate these individuals as lifetime criminals with the constant threat of deportation and family destruction. That approach serves no one. Simply put, they are already here. Let us have a little compassion for these folks, please. We should develop a realistic path to citizenship which is in the best interest of America. Without playing political theater, we need a path which balances the safety of our citizens with the need to successfully integrate these immigrants into our society. Remember the great lady in our harbor:

> *"Give me your tired, your poor, your huddled masses yearning to breathe free."*

These are the very principles of America and these should be the guiding principles of our path to citizenship for all illegal immigrants.

It is true, when an individual illegally immigrates to the United States, the vetting process designed to protect our national security and safety of our citizens is unduly bypassed.

However, more so than any questionnaire, 18th Century test, or vetting process; I believe being a good and constructive member of the community for many years is sufficient to demonstrate the commitment to the United States and our beliefs.

Our approach for path to citizenship should give consideration to the time and duration an individual has been a constructive member of our community, albeit illegally. Specifically if the child under the age of thirteen is illegally brought to the United States (e.g. a Dreamer) that child should become an American citizen on his eighteenth birthday with a Social Security number issued, the right to vote, and the right to serve in our military in defense of our country.

For children above the age of thirteen through adulthood, citizenship should be granted upon successfully demonstrating ten years of constructive participation in our society, while maintaining no serious criminal violations, whatsoever. In both children and adult, this would provide an aspirational goal to positively contribute to our society with the reward of being recognized as a full United States citizen for their commitment to America. Let us once again demonstrate to all the Nations and Peoples of the world that America is a compassionate, kindhearted, and open country of boundless opportunity where all are welcomed.

Jobs & Labor

The working men and women in America have been taking it in the shorts for decades, certainly ever since I have been in the workforce (the early 80's). Multiple macroeconomic factors have been unleashed to gut the American working class, and thus our middle-class. These economic factors have been exacerbated by corporate greed and outsourcing.

After World War II, in the 40's and 50's, it was common place that only one household income was needed to raise a family in a comfortable middle-class standard. Fast-forward to 2017 and now too often, two household incomes are needed just to scrape by. Families are running perilously close to not scraping by at all in the untimely event of an illness, loss of job, or other family emergency. The American dream widely realized by our parents, unfortunately, is becoming less attainable and sustainable for the working class of today. The actual statistics on this reality paint a very bleak picture for our children's future.   According to the findings of "The Equality of Opportunity Project" in 1940, 92% of American children earned more than their parents earned. This meant that children in 1940 could expect a higher standard of living than their parents. Unfortunately, the percentage of children who would ultimately earn more than their parents has continued to drop over the decades; which parallels the fading American Dream. Now less than 50% of American Children born can expect to earn more than their parents. For those who may not know, "The Equality of Opportunity Project" is a large economics research initiative led by notable economist from Harvard, Brown University, Stanford and other prestigious universities. These are the best and brightest in economics.

There are numerous reasons why working class families across this country are struggling to make ends meet. These factors have combined to negatively impact the real wages we can earn as a household. Sadly, many of these causes have been designed by the wealthiest elite to exploit the working class and for no other reason than good old fashion greed. From a macro-economic perspective over the past few decades, wealth has been concentrated in fewer and fewer hands. To illustrate this fact, according to statistics researched by Emmanuel Saez of the University of California, Berkeley and Garbiel Zucman of the

London School of Economics, the richest top 0.1% of American households now owns as much as the bottom 90% households; that's .01% not 1%. This concentration of wealth is staggering. Stop and let this sink in for a bit. A handful of rich individuals in America own as much as 90% of ALL American households combined. Perhaps most troubling, the wealth concentration in America is accelerating and getting worse.

It is alarming that the last time the richest families had such a profound concentration of wealth in America was on the eve of the Great Depression. This is a frightening economic prospect for our future. To date, I have only heard a single very lonesome, forward-thinking, progressive voice on the political landscape that has rightly focused on this disturbing reality of wealth concentration. I won't mention his name here, as I promised to steer clear of referencing any current American politicians. Even though I am not referencing him by name, make no mistake he was absolutely right and should be thanked.

As a result of this extreme wealth concentration, the working men and women of America are earning less inflation adjusted dollars annually, simply because the economic pie continues to shrink. Wealth is continually being taken out of the circulation and concentrated in fewer and fewer hands. This wealth concentration is largely due to "trickle-down" economics which began in the 1980's, as well as generous tax breaks for the rich.

The stark reality of trickle-down economics is in fact it doesn't actually trickle-down to anyone but the rich. Fully 90% of American households never benefit from this type of regressive policy. Conversely, the vast majority of American households are materially hurt financially from this kind of "rich-man's policy". We are seeing this play out in real-time with the current HealthCare debate. Today, a few regressively backwards lawmakers are trying to sneak in a Trillion dollar tax cut for the very wealthy to be paid for quite literally by the blood and lives of the middle and lower class, in the form of reduced health coverage. I have even heard the bandying about of the phrase "trickle-down economics", as justification of the tax-cut for the wealthy in the hope of conning Americans one more time. America for your own safety and security, as well as that of your children and grandchildren, please don't buy this horse manure. Unless you are in the top 1% of wealth in this country, trickle-down economics will hurt your family.

Beyond the concentration of wealth evaporating our potential wages, without a doubt, Technology has dramatically impacted the working class too. While technology certainly makes the workplace more efficient and brings great benefits to life, it does so largely at the expense of the working class in America. For instance, robotics can perform skilled tasks on the factory line or in a mine at a fraction of the cost of numerous human workers. With the exception of routine maintenance the robots can perform 24x7, 365 days a year. A pace human workers simply cannot match individually. As a result, we need fewer workers.

Computers too with their high-speed processing have replaced the need for countless accountants, bookkeepers, tax preparer's, secretaries, and general clerical. Then add in the Internet, and the remaining jobs can now cheaply be done in countries with lower standard of living and less labor law protections. This is the specific reason why so many customer service jobs and technology programming jobs are now being performed overseas for American companies.

While technology has certainly impacted the American work-force, so too has corporate greed. In the 40s, 50s, 60s, and 70s it was quite common for a worker to get a job with a good company and work their entire career with that one company. But beginning in the 80s corporate greed began running amok. Initially it started with new terms, at the time, like "right-sizing" and "downsizing". Corporations would no longer be loyal to a worker simply because they had worked there for 10 or 15 years. At the first opportunity to shave expenses, they would be cut.

Companies began laying off skilled labor with little to no notice. With the previous loyalty from company to worker now a thing of the past, workers sensing the potential loss of security with their current company began changing jobs more frequently. Thus an endless loop of labor destabilization began. After the wave of rightsizing and downsizing had ravaged the American workers, technology enabled outsourcing and still more jobs left America. And with the continual effort to squeeze more profits out of the turnip, corporations introduced the concept of matrix management and flattened the organizational chart even further thus eliminating the role of many middle managers.

One could argue that all of this is merely a function of the capitalistic free-market economy, constantly streamlining, improving, and making processes more efficient. And to some degree, I would agree with that argument. However that argument loses its righteous pontification when you realize that the newly realized profits flowed at a far slower rate to shareholders, while simply not flowing at all to labor. So who got the money?

As we discussed earlier, since the 1980's it is painfully obvious that the disparity of wealth between the rich and poor in America has widened, as the concentration of wealth is aggressively pursued. Certainly, trickle-down economics and tax breaks for the rich contributed largely to this wealth concentration at the expense of working families. But compounding the problem, our economy has been raped by the insatiable profiteering by the C-Suite of Corporate America, the handful of ordained nobility at every company. The C-Suite Executives are the muckety-mucks who don't bother even saying "good morning" to you as you pass them in the elevator.

Today, it is not uncommon for CEO of a major corporation in America to make well over $50 million per year. Contrast that with the reality that a minimum-wage worker in America at that same Corporation would earn only $15,000 a year. This means that the CEO, his buddies on the board, and C-suite, values his worth at approximately 3,333 times more than the minimum wage worker. Another way to look at it, today a minimum wage worker would have to work for more than three thousand years to earn what the CEO earned in just one year. Sound fair? I guess it sounds fair if you are fortunate enough to be in the 1%, but for the rest of us 99% schmucks, not so much.

I have met a lot of C-Suite Executives over the years and frankly most of them are about, as worthless as, hen poop on a pump handle. These folks are neither Einsteins nor clairvoyant economic sooth-sayers. They quite literally are no smarter or more insightful than the common worker on the factory line. They just get paid a helluva lot more than the line worker. Most of these C-Suite Executives got placed on top of the heap by who they knew, who they married, or being born into an affluent wealthy family. There is nothing unique or special about these individuals. Remember, they all wake up in the morning and wipe their backsides the same as you and me.

And to date, I have never in my life witnessed any man who is worth more than 3,000 times that of another man, certainly not a C-Suite Executive. The annual salaries and bonuses of the C-Suite are out of control, as they are in charge of the purse strings. Annual salary raises in the C-Suite often exceed 15-20% while the working class wages are often directly tied to the annual inflation rate, approximately 2.25% today. This means that the working class is effectively earning the same amount of money (inflation adjusted dollars) that they did the previous year. Not to even mention the prevailing wage disparity between men and women performing the exact same job. This is intolerable, insufferable, and flat ass wrong.

I am a supporter of the capitalist free-market system when it benefits everyone and not a handful of greedy C-Suite profiteers. To help rectify this widening chasm of economic disparity, we not only need to increase the minimum salary to a livable wage of $15 per hour, but simultaneously introduce a maximum wage that ties the highest paid executive in any corporation directly to the wages of the lowest paid worker at the same company. This relationship should be no more than 100:1, executive compensation to the company minimum wage. We need to ensure that the C-Suite Executives have a vested interest in the common worker succeeding in America. There is no better way to do this than tie their fortunes together.

At a minimum livable rate of $15 per hour, a working husband and wife could expect to earn a combined minimum of $60,000 per year to raise their family. This would still entitle the CEO to earn 100 times more than the minimum wage earner for that company or roughly, $3,000,000 per year. There would be no limit on how much a CEO could earn at a corporation, other than it would be tied to the lowest wage paid at the corporation. If the CEO wants to make more money than $3,000,000, great, raise the wage of the lowest worker and the CEO could then raise their wage accordingly. If we did this, corporate profits would begin to flow more towards both investors and labor, with less accumulation in the C-Suite. A rising economic tide should lift all boats not just the yachts, which is the environment we have today.

Beyond raising the minimum wage to a livable wage in America and directly tying the highest paid executive to the lowest paid common worker, we need to de-incentivize the value of outsourcing, so it is no longer pursued at the expense of the American worker. The way this could be achieved is by adding an outsourcing corporate tax to every outsourced job equal to the cost of the current regulatory enacted protections of the American worker. For example if we have a minimum-wage in our country, then the outsourced worker must be calculated at the same minimum-wage; a mandatory 40 hour work week would need to be observed, as well, as child labor laws; and pertinent unemployment insurances and Social Security costs factored in. In doing this we can level set the economic playing field between American workers and outsourced workers that do not have the same rights, regulatory protections, or labor guarantees. This would stop corporate greed from exploiting our workers by outsourcing jobs away from America.

We are not in a position to force a foreign government to enact similar labor protection regulations equal to our own, though they should. However within America, we certainly can prevent American companies from exploiting these regulatory labor differences at the cost of the American worker. Likewise, we could prevent foreign companies from exploiting these same regulatory labor differences, while selling products in America by increasing import tariffs on products manufactured abroad. The tariffs would not apply if the products were manufactured and assembled in America.

Not only should America de-incent companies from outsourcing, we should provide clear and compelling incentives (e.g. lower taxes, credits, and rebates) for companies to re-patriot jobs to economically distressed regions in America. This would benefit all of America by lifting whole regions out of poverty. In doing so we would create organic demand for goods and products, as more Americans would now be able to afford these products. This organic demand would spur significant economic growth; similar to the boom we experienced post WWII, when returning GI's were able to afford a house in the suburbs.

This is a bottom-up economics approach, which is the only sustainable economic model. We have long heard the supposed promise of trickle-down economics, where ultimately everyone would benefit if the richest people benefitted first. This is a myth. Supposedly the rich will benefit, and then they will turn their profits into additional investments in the economy. Reality is when the rich benefit financially; they simply begin hoarding the monies. These monies are seldom invested directly back into the American economy. This is why trickle-down economics is a fanciful, fairytale meant to lull the gullible populace into giving more of their hard-earned money to the rich. This is one of the contributing reasons for the ever widening economic disparity between the haves and have-nots.

In a bottom-up economics model, broad-based demand is built across society for goods, products, and services. It is this new demand that will ultimately drive new jobs, new technologies, and new efficiencies, as companies strive to meet the new demand. This creates a positive, reinforcing, and self-sustaining, economic model. Everyone in the economy benefits from bottom-up economics. In contrast, only the super-rich benefit by trickle-down economics.

The last topic we need to touch on regarding jobs and labor is the ever present glass ceiling in America. This invisible barrier preventing women from advancing was contrived by men, as a not so subtle form of discrimination. Though not seen, this barrier is very real. This concept of a glass ceiling is nothing more than males exerting dominance over females and thus "keeping the li'l woman in her place, barefoot and pregnant".

The unseen glass ceiling prevents women from ascending to the top levels of organizations and exists throughout America; whether in Academia, Corporate America, HealthCare, or even Government. It's indelibly dyed in a dirty little myth that women cannot handle important jobs of consequence. Unconscionable excuses are routinely tossed out by men as justifications for keeping this invisible barrier; "women may get pregnant", "they may menstruate", and of course "women are certainly too emotional and hysterical to handle any leadership role". All of which are absolutely and categorically wrong.

This is a societal problem in America that we need to address if we are ever going to advance as a country. Women constantly have to break thru this glass ceiling to new levels simply to have their voices heard; only to find a new glass ceiling placed above them again. As a society by continuing to ignore the talents, skills, and leadership of half of our population, we are inadvertently short changing our country's potential. Really after two hundred and forty years of history, America has still never found a woman sufficiently qualified to be president? This is pathologically ridiculous. Why is it that numerous countries across history have been very successfully led by women but not here in America? The fact is that America is woefully backwards and inept on this topic.

The perpetuation of the glass ceiling is reinforced constantly by both overt and subtle actions. We can see the glass ceiling being invoked in the pay gaps that exist between men and women for the same job. We also see the invisible barrier applied to prevent women from consideration for various leadership roles. They are quietly passed over and never considered. The glass ceiling is present on the floor of the US Senate when a male Senator interrupts a female senator and prevents her from voicing her opinion or during Senate hearings when a male Senator dismisses the concerns of a female Senator. This invisible barrier even exists during high profile political campaigns, as candidates have slurred vulgar, indecent, and belittling insults against women to minimize their gender.

I find the very notion of a glass-ceiling to be unequivocally unjustifiable. Remember, every single American wouldn't be here if not for being born by a woman. Women comprise more than 50% of our population. They are our mothers, wives, sisters, and partners. Are we as a society willing to discriminate against half of our population; our mothers, wives, and sisters? Are we as a society willing to deny ourselves the potential that these women can bring to America if only permitted to do so? I hope as a country, we can wake up and remove all of these invisible barriers today.

Military and Veteran Affairs

Unabashedly, I love our military. I have absolute respect, admiration, and appreciation for the men and women who selflessly serve our nation. These are truly the sons and daughters of America. Gen. Norman Schwarzkopf said in best:

"You should never forget that the airplanes don't fly, the tanks don't run, the ships don't sail, and the missiles don't fire unless the sons and daughters of America make them do it"

I very much appreciate this recognition and sentiment by such an important Military Commander and US Hero. I came from a family of Marines. My dad was wounded in Korea, most of my brothers served, and I served as well. Given our close ties to the military, I view our servicemen and women, as extended family. It is critical to remember every single man and woman that serves in our military is somebody's child, brother, sister, or spouse. Too often our leaders conveniently forget this fact and are far too cavalier to committing our troops into harm's way without clearly defined strategic objectives and plans. These judgement errors by our leaders cost America dearly in both lives and taxpayers dollars. Even when we do originally have clearly defined objectives, our leaders often change or morph the original goals to serve their own political purposes.

Case in point, remember why the United States first invaded Afghanistan and Pakistan in 2001? In the wake of 9/11, America wanted to kill or capture Osama bin Laden, the leader of al-Qaida and the reported mastermind of the terrorist attack. US intelligence indicated that bin Laden was being harbored and aided by the Taliban in the mountains of Afghanistan and Pakistan. Given the attack on America, I believe this was entirely justified to bring this terrorist monster to justice. We finally tracked bin Laden down a decade later in his compound in Abbottabad, Pakistan and killed him on May 2, 2011. On that day, we accomplished our mission. So why is it exactly in 2017, we are still embroiled in the longest war in US History with no end in sight if we accomplished our original goal six years ago?

According to the *Costs of War Study* (Brown University, Watson Institute International and Public Affairs), the wars in Afghanistan, Pakistan, Iraq, and Syria have resulted in 370,000 deaths with 6,800 deaths being from our US Military, America's sons and daughters. The Brown University Study determined that American taxpayers have spent $3.7 trillion though 2016 with an additional $1.1 trillion in projected future cost. Obviously, this is a huge cost to America especially when you consider that we successfully accomplished our mission several years ago and we as a country are currently $20 trillion in debt.

When we first started the war in Afghanistan our mission was crystal clear, kill or capture Osama bin Laden. Now our mission is much less clear, if existent at all. We have no defined clear objective other than hunt through every canyon and cave looking for the "bad guys" behind every rock. The problem is in the past 16 years young militant extremist from around the world have flocked to Afghanistan for the opportunity to shoot at the so-called American infidels. As a result, the only thing we are really accomplishing today is taking Afghanistan rubble and simply making smaller rubble out of it. This is a pointless exercise and certainly not worth the lives of our soldiers.

Gen. Schwarzkopf knew the value of our soldier's lives. He was obsessed; rightly so, with minimizing US causalities during the first Gulf War even when he was squaring off against a formidable Iraqi force of 300,000 battle hardened soldiers and 2,000 tanks. The Iraqi dictator Saddam Hussein's goal was to inflict as many American casualties as possible to deter America from intervening in his conquest of Kuwait. Hussein's threatening rhetoric bore witness to his horrifying intentions:

~ *"The Mother of all Battles"*

~ *"Yours is a society which cannot accept 10,000 dead in one battle."*

~ *"The dawn of victory nears as this great showdown begins...The evil and satanic intentions of the White House will be crushed and so will all the blasphemous and oppressive forces."*

Even with this as the back drop for the First Gulf War, as a direct result of Schwarzkopf's meticulous plans, our Military Technology advantage, and of course our soldier's bravery resulted in minimal loss to America. US military had (235) deaths in the conflict theater compared to tens of thousands of Iraqi deaths. In addition, the First Gulf war is notably the cheapest war in US history at only .3% of our GDP (1991). We had a clear objective and superior planning with the emphasis on reducing American causalities; a winning strategy.

As a country, we should never ask the sons and daughters of America, as well as, our American families to bear the ultimate sacrifice in battle if we don't first have a clearly defined objective, strategy, and mission in place. These no longer exist in Afghanistan and Pakistan. As we accomplished our stated mission in 2011, it serves no US strategic purpose for our troops to remain in Afghanistan or Pakistan today other than our ego. If we withdrew our military forces from this region, we could potentially save several hundred billion tax dollars annually not to mention thousands of US lives.

We should avoid placing "boots on the ground" as the very last possible option and only after all other options have been exhausted. Obviously, I would favor diplomatic solutions whenever/wherever a conflict arises. Unfortunately, it is a reality that diplomatic solutions are not always attainable or even realistic. In those unique situations, I would prefer to intervene first through technology whether that is jamming of technologies, infrastructure disruption, drones, missile strikes, or even strategic bombings. However, we should always attempt to minimize our soldier's exposure to harm; fighting on the battlefield and timing of our choice not that of our enemies. Lastly, once our originally defined strategies are accomplished, we should immediately withdraw our forces and avoid prolonged costly engagements, which undermine America's credibility to the rest of the world.

There is always a lot of debate around "who" should be allowed to join our military and fight for America; whether women, homosexuals, transgender, various religions, or races should be permitted. I would answer that question quite simply; ALL American citizens should be permitted the right to serve our country with distinction. And please don't talk to me about "Esprit de Corps"; remember I come from a family of Marines. America is a diverse country and our military, throughout all ranks, should clearly reflect that diversity.

While the opportunity to serve our country should be open to all American citizens, we cannot turn a blind eye or deaf ear to protecting these soldier's human rights while in our service. No service member should endure discrimination, sexual assault, or harassment simply because of their sex, race, religion, or orientation. Stiff penalties need to exist within our military for any such violations throughout the chain of command. Stiffer penalties need to be enforced on any commander or ranking officer who does not aggressively pursue a zero tolerance of these violations. The recent baseless political attack on our transgender servicemen and women is shameful and should be overturned immediately by Congress.

After our citizens have served America, it is our turn to serve them and pay them back for their contributions. Veteran's benefits are an absolute necessity and I am a very strong proponent of all of these. Today the United States provides a myriad of benefits to these most deserving citizens. The benefits for our Veterans include Disability Compensation, Education & Training, Life Insurance, Home Loans, HealthCare, Dependent & Survivor Benefits, and even Burial. While the bulk of our Veterans Benefits are well thought out and executed, I personally believe we are failing our veterans regarding our promise for HealthCare in both quality of care and access to care. Sadly, it is not uncommon for veterans to wait months or even years to be seen by a specialist through the VA. Most sadly, some of our hero-veterans have even succumbed to their ailments long before being seen. This is unacceptable.

By leveraging the previously discussed Universal HealthCare system, we could immediately address the wanting deficiencies in our Veteran's HealthCare, improve their access, and overall care. In consideration of their service to our country, Veteran's monthly cost for the Universal HealthCare System would be waived. They would enjoy full access to all medical providers, labs, devices and prescriptions at no cost without having to go through the VA. The associated VA Medical Budget would be used as an offset to the cost of providing Universal HealthCare to our veterans.

Robert Marks

National Defense

The safety and national defense of America simply is not matched or even remotely approached by any other country in the world. From a national defense perspective America without a doubt is the most secure country in the world. America's physical geographical position in North America contributes to this security. Bordered by Canada, Mexico, and the Atlantic & Pacific Oceans, physical invasion of our country by anyone is a very distant and remote possibility. In addition to our geographical location, America's national defense is further secured by our tolerant democratic political system, free market economy, and the greatest military the world has ever known.

Today there is not a country in the world that I would fear could legitimately invade the United States of America. Though there are a few countries around the world that do still present a threat to our security and safety, albeit not an invasion threat. We do have lesser vulnerabilities to our national defense. These vulnerabilities in and of themselves would not be capable of bringing down the United States, however they certainly could cause significant disruptions, potential loss of life, and significant economic cost and impact.

Perhaps the greatest and most immediate single threat we have today to our national defense is that of wide spread cyber-attacks. With the proliferation of technology and the Internet, every computer in the world is vulnerable to attacks. As we are by far the most technically advanced nation in the world, we likewise are the most vulnerable to potential attack. These cyber-attacks can be sponsored by any number of bad actors in the world and are difficult to defend against.

Several countries (e.g. Russia, China, North Korea, etc.) routinely engage in both cyber espionage and cyber sabotage. This was most recently demonstrated by Russia's successful attempts to hack our presidential elections. Even when countries are not directly attacking us as Russia did, they are often engaged in stealing technology and intellectual property through high-tech espionage, costing our Government and Corporations billions annually. Even beyond state sponsored cyber-attacks, organized crime throughout the world has recently begun distributing ransom-ware in order to blackmail large corporations, hospitals, and power grids with the threat of losing their data. This is in addition to their relentless theft of consumer confidential data and sale on the black market. Terrorist organizations are likewise continuing to probe for weaknesses in our infrastructure and transportation networks. If all of these groups constantly attacking the US technology and computers were not enough, you can add in good old-fashioned lone wolf anti-social hackers into the mix as well.

Although cyber-attacks are difficult to defend against, we do need a tightly coordinated and well-funded governmental effort to counter this ongoing threat to our national security. Depending on the specific attack, American lives could be at stake if Hospitals, Rail, Air Traffic, Satellite, or our Power Grid were significantly disrupted. Unfortunately, we are very vulnerable to these attacks today and must take immediately action to address our vulnerabilities. To remove needless bureaucratic delays in our responsiveness to cyber threats, the US National Cyber Security Division (NCSD) should be elevated to a cabinet post and funded accordingly.

As everyone in America is aware since 9/11, another clear and present threat to our national security is well funded and organized international terrorist attacks. While we may be limited somewhat in preventing lone-wolf, poorly organized, impromptu, individual attacks in the US, we should be better at preventing or disrupting the well-organized and well-funded terrorist attacks orchestrated from abroad.

When we speak about well-funded and organized foreign terrorists, I believe there's a clear link, both direct and indirect, to the commoditization of oil for their funding. Please note fully (15) individuals who carried out the September 11th terrorist attack against America were from Saudi Arabia (supposedly our ally), while (2) attackers were from the United Arab Emirates, (1) from Lebanon, and (1) from Egypt. Osama bin Laden himself had ties to the Saudi royal family and its vast oil revenues.

Iran the world's fifth largest producer of oil was cited recently as the world's biggest state sponsor of terrorism on February 4, 2017 by the United States Defense Secretary. In addition, ISIS has funded its aggressive expansion and territorial gains directly through oil proceeds. While I certainly don't believe that every barrel of oil produced in the world goes directly to terrorism, there is an undeniable link between oil and terrorism in the world. Many of the countries that fund (overtly or covertly) terrorism have no other mentionable products for export other than sand and oil. Obviously, sand does not command much money on the open market, so they inevitably turn to oil to fund their terrorist goals.

In the past twenty years, we have heard a lot from politicians from both parties about the supposed "war on terrorism". It is evident; we do not have a long-range strategy for defeating terrorism. But rather we have engaged in numerous reactionary tactics to combat terrorism wherever we find it. When I say reactionary, I'm specifically talking about the Wars in Iraq, Afghanistan, Syria or any other hotbeds of terrorist activity that we quickly deploy our troops to and then camp out for many years at enormous cost of lives and money to the tax payers. This is not a strategy but rather political knee-jerk tactics; deploying our troops across broad swaths of territories to ferret the terrorist out of their caves. Frankly, we will never win the war against terrorism this way, as we are fighting against cultures, similar to what happened in Vietnam.

In lieu of this haphazard reactionary approach, I prefer a much more strategic and overarching long term approach to defeating terrorism globally, specifically by cutting their common supply line. The common supply line that is funding terrorist expansion, recruitment, and hostilities globally is the commodity of oil. Whether we recognize it or not, every time an American purchases a gallon of gasoline, we are unwittingly creating additional demand for oil and petroleum products worldwide. This continued demand for oil globally is commoditized by various nefarious groups and directly/indirectly funds terrorist activities.

Instead of deploying troops to every terrorist hotspot like playing a crazy game of military whack-a-mole, my goal to defeat terrorism would be to declare war against oil, break American economic dependency on oil, and deplete terrorist of needed oil revenues. Obviously, this won't happen in a year. However with concerted political will and effort, which we lack today, it very well could take 10-20 years to successfully implement such a strategy.

While that seems like a very distant time in the future, remember 9/11 happened sixteen years ago. Had we pursued this strategy at that time, we would be much further along in defeating global terrorism today and denying terrorist the resources to operate. Yes, we have killed Osama Bin Laden, Fahid Mohammed Ally Msalam, Fazul Abdullah Mohammed, and countless other terrorist during the past twenty years. Even so global terrorism is still spreading in Africa, Europe, and Philippines and we are embroiled in multiple costly wars simultaneously. As soon as we kill one terrorist leader, another "Bin Laden wanna-be" takes their place. We have to change our tactics and adopt a long term strategy if we are to prevail in this war against global terrorism.

Specifically, I want to devalue and de-commoditize oil globally, such that oil becomes, as worthless as sand. This would ultimately undercut terrorist funding across the world. Again remember the states that are sponsoring terrorism have limited other mentionable commodity alternatives to export. America on the other hand has the ultimate commodity to export, food and grain; which will always be in high demand. Once we fully devalue oil globally and break its stranglehold on America, we can have a very constructive conversation with the various oil producing terrorist states.

If we are serious as a nation about protecting our national defense and winning the so-called "war against terrorism" than we must first declare war against oil and thus eliminate the terrorist funding at its source. Beyond terrorist leveraging oil as their principle funding mechanism (directly or indirectly), it is important to note that America is currently dependent on other nations for 60% of all oil we consume. This is not a good strategic position. Simply put, America does not control our own destiny when it comes to our addiction to oil. As a nation, how many conflicts and wars have we been drawn into over the past fifty years under the ever present claim of "America's National Interest"? The national interest is of course little more than oil, preserving our access, and national addiction to it. It is not a question of "who" provides us the oil or can we provide it ourselves by destroying the environment. The question is "how do we eliminate oil from any and all usage in the United States, regardless of which country provides it?" All fossil fuels are finite and non-renewable, they will eventually run out. Our National Defense hangs in the balance. Today, we are hostages.

We are the world's largest consumer of oil, if we can develop alternative fuels that make oil obsolete it would devastate oil demand globally. Once we successfully develop and implement the alternative fuels through our economy, we should share this technology with the rest of the industrialized nations. Again, the strategic goal to defeating terrorism is to devalue and de-commoditize oil by eliminating global demand. Thus we would cut the terrorist financial supply line and cripple their capacity to operate, while simultaneously strengthening America's independence and by the way, reducing carbon emissions and Global warming.

Beyond cyber-attacks and global terrorism, the opioid and heroin epidemic directly threatens our national security. The New York Times reported on June 5, 2017 that drug overdoses are now the leading cause of death in America for those under 50 years old. The article continued with preliminary data indicating that over 59,000 Americans died from drug overdose in 2016. This number is significantly higher than the number of gun related deaths, HIV deaths, or even deaths from Car Accidents for any single year. This is considerably more than have ever died from terrorist attacks in the United States. To put this into perspective, the 59,000 Americans who died from drug overdose in 2016 roughly equates to the total American military deaths during fourteen years of the Vietnam War. Now do I have your attention? America has a serious problem on our hands.

I simply do not believe that locking addicts away for long prison sentences is the answer. This is an extremely costly proposition and does little more than warehouse an addict until they get out of prison. This approach does not remotely address the underlying psychological issues which are driving the individual to addiction. In addition locking addicts away causes irreparable harm to families. I have no problem locking away drug dealers and traffickers; however we have to address the root psychological issues associated with the addicts in order to break the demand.

On January 12 2017 the Los Angeles Times reported about just such a unique approach to address the root psychological issues associated with addiction. The creative approach was taken in Switzerland in the early 2000's and shows great promise. Switzerland had been dealing with its own opiate epidemic, rather unsuccessfully similar to the United States. What the Swiss came up with a very compassionate balancing routine. Recognizing that the opiate users were physically dependent and addicted to the drug, the addict would pursue the drug relentlessly. This translated into higher crimes, prostitution, and violence directly impacting society. The addicts were unable to break the grip of their dependency without both extensive psychological and physical support.

The Swiss program addresses both of these fundamental needs for the addict. The addicts are provided the necessary opiates in a clean medical center under the supervision of nursing and medical staff free of charge. This takes the attics directly off the street and out of the reach of the dealers, while depriving the dealers of needed customer demand for their product. It's very hard for a dealer to compete with free product. In exchange for the free opiates the patients agree to psychological support and counseling to help break the addiction. Overtime the patients are slowly and methodically stepped down from their addiction, with the necessary support. The patient can remain in the program as long as needed. This program seems like a much more reasonable and compassionate approach to combat the opioid epidemic.

Robert Marks

North Korea

Here is a thorny issue for sure. The Democratic People's Republic of Korea, a.k.a. North Korea, is a frightening, aggressive, destabilizing, & unpredictable country in Far East Asia. The term "Democratic" is in name only.   This is a totalitarian communist country. Three generations of twisted psychopathic despots have mercilessly ruled this country, subjugated its citizens, and continuously threatened their neighbors. Most notably South Korea and Japan have been in the crosshairs of the unpredictable North Korean regime. Today, North Korea is a diplomatic pariah on the world stage, as they have promoted, supported, and exported global terrorism and pursued development of long-range nuclear weapons.

North Korea's aggressive behavior began after WWII when Kim Il-Sung wrongly predicted that a war weary world and specifically the United Nations would not intervene in a military conflict on the Korean Peninsula. Backed by considerable Soviet armor and artillery, Kim Il-Sung rolled the dice. North Korea invaded South Korea by surprise and crossed the 38th parallel. The North Korean armies nearly succeeded before a host of United Nations countries forced the North back across the 38th parallel and nearly all the way to the Chinese Border. This compelled the Chinese to act fearing potential invasion of their homeland and they helped the North Koreans push the UN forces back to the original border.

The border between the two Koreas solidified around the 38th parallel with the signing of an armistice. This created a demilitarized zone (DMZ) between the two Koreas. The border between the two Koreas today is the heaviest militarized border in the world. It is notable that North Korea has never accepted a peace treaty with South Korea. Thus the two Koreas are technically still at war, a rather unsettling fact and predicament.

This aggressive bellicose behavior from the North continued when Kim Il-Sung's son Kim Jong-Il took control. He furthered ties with China continued his saber rattling with his neighbor to the south and began to export terrorism globally to the highest bidder. Kim Jong-Il was succeeded by his son Kim Jong-Un, who was born in 1984 and is only 33 years old. Given the history of his grandfather and father before him, North Korea has been punished with crippling economic sanctions by the world community. China today is her only economic lifeline. We need to compel China to exercise their influence over North Korea to help resolve current conflicts in humanity's interest.

There is great distrust by the North Korean regime of any Democratic liberties or freedoms. They believe that the Korea Peninsula should be unified under the North Korean, communist flag. It is for this reason and perceived self-preservation that North Korea has relentlessly pursued long-range nuclear weapons. Perhaps the North feels that if they own a bomb they will elevate their status in the world. However given the history of the three North Korean regimes since World War II, a nuclear capable North Korea is a near death sentence to both South Korea and Japan. Both South Korea and Japan are peaceful nations pursuing democratic ideals and strong economies.

So what exactly can the United States or even the world do to prevent this reckless regime from garnering weapons of mass destruction? I believe a limited military strike to disable the nuclear capabilities of North Korea is ill advised and frankly a short-term solution. Even if a strike was successful and it did not provoke retaliation from either China or Russia, North Korea would undoubtedly pursue nuclear capabilities with renewed vigor.

North Korea

I would like to see a longer-term, diplomatic solution for the North Korea problem. I don't believe that negotiating directly with a maniac would be productive. So that removes the possibility of a direct conversation with North Korea. Nor would I want to elevate the North Korean despot to the level of a legitimate world leader. I believe any diplomatic negotiation would have to be collectively with the People's Republic of China, Russia, Japan, and South Korea by necessity, as these countries are under the gravest immediate risk. While China is a nuclear capable communist nation, it has been a very stable and predictable country in the world and has not sought to aggressively dominate its neighbors by military expanse. The same cannot be said for Russia (e.g. Ukraine, etc.). While Human Rights in China are certainly a legitimate concern, I would hazard that the current Human Rights environment in North Korea is far worse by comparison.

The line of negotiations, I would pursue with the direct neighbors of North Korea would be a Multi-lateral Treaty with the stated goal of a regime change in North Korea. The Treaty would need to be validated by the direct neighbors of North Korea, as well as, the United Nations. This Treaty would have the purpose of collectively dissolving the Government of the Democratic People's Republic of Korea, while transitioning this region to China for direct governance & oversight for a period of 100 years. The time duration of the treaty for China to govern North Korea, would be similar to the Panama Canal treaty with the United States controlling the canal territory several years before handing it back to the country of Panama. The Treaty would need to have a military component by all the neighboring countries and United Nations to enforce the Treaty and quickly deal with any aggressive counter actions taken by North Korea, both of which would be likely and foreseeable. This is another reason why an overwhelming multilateral military component would be a necessity.

After achieving the goal of the treaty, North Korea would remain a communist nation under the control of the People's Republic of China. While not removing the Nuclear threat from the peninsula, as China is already nuclear enabled, the world would gain a much more stable and predictable country to deal with going forward. This would reduce the overall threat and eminent likelihood of a nuclear war on the Korean Peninsula. China simply may not want the headache of taking on and governing North Korea for 100 years. But in consideration for taking on this headache of governing North Korea, the Treaty would also affect the One-China policy. Specifically, the Multi-lateral Treaty would transition the sovereignty and control of

Taiwan returning this Island nation back to the original homeland of China, becoming fully effective again in 100 years. This would provide more than adequate time for decapitalizing investments on the island if desired or the emigration of citizens seeking to leave the island altogether.

Yes, I understand Taiwan is today a democratic country, though very recent in history. However, historically before the Sino Japanese War (1894-1895) Taiwan has been a part of China. A Treaty ending the first Sino Japanese war transitioned Taiwan to Japan for a brief period. At the end of WWII the Japanese surrendered Taiwan back to China.

The timing of the Japanese surrender of the island of Taiwan is somewhat problematic. When Japan surrendered the island back to China, there was actually a Civil War taking place in China with no clear victor at this point. Before WWII (1927-1937) the Chinese Civil War raged between the Chinese Communist led by Mao Tse-tung and the corrupt and oppressive Republic of China (ROC) government, led by Generalissimo Chiang Kai-shek. This civil war moderated somewhat during WWII years as both sides fought against Japanese aggression.

Immediately following WWII 1945-1949 the civil war hostilities between the Communist and ROC forces soon resumed and concluded with the rout of Generalissimo Chiang

Kai-shek ROC army across Mainland China by the communist. Chiang Kai-shek's government (Republic of China) fled to the Island of Taiwan, where he persecuted and subjugated the population; not a nice guy. It wasn't until the mid-1980s, after the death of Chiang, that Taiwan began to democratize. This effort was mostly out of self-preservation and to better align with the United States against China.

However from a historical perspective, China's fortune was largely decided in 1949 by popular Chinese demand. So too the fortune of Taiwan should have been decided at that same time, as China is the legitimate owner of the island. Generalissimo Chiang Kai-shek was a corrupt murderous thug, and Taiwan should be returned to China through a smooth transition process.

Should only three of the four neighbors of North Korea (People's Republic of China, Russia, Japan, and South Korea) agree to the Treaty and dissolve the North Korean government, which would be sufficient to act with the approval of the United Nations. If however only two of the four neighbors agreed, we would be forced to take a more direct action with less reliance and dependency on the military assistance of North Korea's neighbors. The mission again would be removing the North Korean leader's regime in an attempt to introduce more stability to the region. We would need to sever the head of the serpent. I have heard the old saying "better to deal with the devil you know", but seriously I rather doubt at this point that it would be humanly possible to introduce less stability to the peninsula.

I would <u>strongly</u> prefer to work towards a multi-lateral partnership and regional solution with North Korea's direct neighbors. However, if this is simply un-attainable or proves not to be realistic, then we should consider both a "highly targeted" Special Forces action or if necessary a wide ranging pre-emptive strike targeting Senior Command and Control Infrastructure. While certainly not palatable, given the history and temperament of the North Korean regime, it would be a dire mistake for America if we permitted North Korea to gain a long range nuclear ballistic missile. Currently, they have attained a long range missile capable of striking most of the United States, which could be nuclear enabled within twelve months. If this happens, millions of Americans from San Francisco to New York would be in immediate and imminent peril. This peril would far outweigh potential American losses associated with a comprehensive pre-emptive strike. The principle concern of a pre-emptive strike is that any such action must be absolutely decisive, devastating, complete, and extensive to eliminate any potential counter retaliatory military move by North Korea.

Robert Marks

PACs, Lobbyist, & other Cockroaches

Genesis 1:26 tells us that man has dominion *"over every creeping thing that creepeth upon the earth."* There is simply no slimier *"creeping thing that creepeth upon the earth"* more so than PACs and Lobbyist. These cockroaches are infesting the very cupboards of America's Democracy. We need to exercise our dominion over this pestilence. If you want to know what is wrong with Washington D.C., you need look no further than these two groups of power peddlers.

Dripping with cash, our drooling elected officials queue up to coddle their ubiquitous influence, favor, and gratuitous donations. There is way too much easy cash in our political system and our elected officials are literally addicted to it. Some legislatures want the cash for the next upcoming re-election campaign so they can keep their cushy job, while others simply want the cash for less noble pursuits. The PACs and Lobbyist are well aware of our Legislators insatiable addiction to cash and like any low-life crack dealer they dole out an endless supply to keep them hooked. As a result our political environment is so completely corrupt, our members of Congress today wrongly view PACs and Lobbyist as their only constituents, in lieu of the US Citizens who actually cast their vote.

As a country we desperately need to eliminate the influence of PAC's and Lobbyist, as well as Corporations, in our democracy and return it to our citizens, the men and women who actually built this country, fought, pay their taxes, and vote. We have had a few well intentioned legislative efforts since Watergate to reign in such inappropriate influence in our democracy. The Federal Election Campaign Act of 1971 and the Bipartisan Campaign Reform Act of 2002 focused principally on campaigns. Neither Act has been sufficient to curb the influence of PACs or Lobbyist. I would like to address the issue aggressively through a combination of Legislation and good ol' fashion public pressure. The end goal would be to eliminate the influence of both PAC's and Lobbyist in our political system and deliver America back to our forgotten citizens; the everyday common men and women of our country.

We need our elected officials (and their staff) to come clean on who exactly they are meeting with every waking hour of the day. Are they filling their day by meeting with various corrupt Lobbyist and PACs or are they filling their day meeting with good and decent everyday citizens? We need absolute transparency to our elected officials calendars, meetings, and phone calls. This information needs to be published daily with details of who they are meeting with and the subject of the meeting. The goal here is to ensure that no elected official or their staff ever meets directly with either Lobbyist or PACs. The elected official should only meet with their constituents, other elected officials, or government staff. Immediate and overwhelming public pressure should be applied to any elected official who meets with either Lobbyist or PAC representatives.

The next step we need to do is to pass legislation which would prohibit all Lobbying efforts of any elected official (or their staff) by any individual performing such activities in consideration of receiving any monies whatsoever. No more "Pay for Play". We need to criminalize professional lobbyist and rid them from our political system. I certainly have no problem with citizens contacting their Congress representative to express their personal concerns, but they need to do it as an independent citizen and not while being paid a PAC Salary pushing PAC agendas, which may not align with the voting constituent's best interest. We need to ensure that paid Lobbyist are completely barred from any contact whatsoever with any elected or appointed official. In addition, we should publically publish the name of any individual convicted of "Lobbying for Pay", as we do sex offenders and prostitutes; publishing their name, home address, their employer, their salary, and their employers address with a Scarlet "L".

As far as PACs, these organizations have very deep pockets and are often financed by wealthy individuals, major corporations, or unions. These political groups file under IRS Section 527 (26 U.S.C. § 527) for tax exemption and are commonly known as 527's. Some of the groups do not "expressly advocate" for the election of a specific candidate or party. In doing so these groups skirt being regulated under state or federal campaign finance laws, as well; clever cockroaches.

IRS Section 527 was originally designed to help legitimate Political Parties and candidates running for elected office by eliminating the associated tax burden of reporting monies raised as income. However, today 527's are the domain of the PACs and Super PAC's. While campaign finance law limits how much money individuals may directly contribute to a campaign, there are no upward limits to how much an individual may contribute to a group registered as a 527, nor are there any spending limits imposed. As a result very wealthy individuals exploit this fact to make large contributions to favorite 527 organizations. Monies exceeding what could be otherwise donated to a direct political campaign. Even though PACs are not campaigns, they act like them by crafting and running aggressive attack ads for candidates; again skirting the campaign finance laws.

As I mentioned, I am all about taking power and influence away from PACs, lobbyists, and corporations in America, while rightfully returning it to the hard working citizens of the United States. As citizens, if we are serious about retaking control of our country and wrestling it from the grips of the elitist few; then we should strongly consider repealing IRS Section 527 (26 U.S.C. § 527). At minimum, we should prohibit PACs from filing under Section 527 for tax exemption benefits.

There is no more direct or instantaneous path to reducing the never ending sea of corrupting cash in American politics other than eliminating the tax-free status of Section 527 PAC organizations, which are currently receiving these political contributions. I mentioned earlier under the Federal Income Tax section that we needed to close tax loopholes of the very rich; the tax-exempt status of Section 527 is just one of these loopholes. Rescinding Section 527 for PACs will literally take the punch bowl (e.g. cold hard cash) away from the party. And any elected official, who doesn't whole heartedly support rescinding Section 527 for PACs, should summarily be voted out of office.

Privacy

I have bad news for everyone. If you're looking for me to confirm the existence of Santa Claus, the Tooth Fairy or the Easter Bunny; they don't really exist. For that matter neither does your privacy. The term privacy is more of a concept of rightful ownership. Specifically that an individual has personal knowledge, data, or information that they may or may not wish to share with others. Thus, the information is "private" to them.

People today often believe that personal privacy still does somehow magically exist in our digital age. Perhaps it's comforting to have this feeling of presumed security and invincibility. However, it is definitely a misplaced belief. The only expectation that a person should have today for privacy is that their digital footprint (e.g. SSN, Credit Cards, Photos, Web Browsing, etc.) is a washed in an ocean of other information/data and the ever present carnivorous, opportunistic shark may simply not be in your immediate vicinity. If they were, you would be little more than a tasty fresh snack.

How exactly did we come to this new reality? Technology has always diminished privacy. As far back as quill and parchment, the Gutenberg press, or telegraph; technology has continually eroded privacy. In the past few decades, the advent of high-speed computer processors, the World Wide Web, corporate outsourcing, and of course corporate greed have conspired to eliminate the very notion of privacy; to the point that a realistic expectation of privacy no longer exists.

The proliferation of the World Wide Web means that data criminals now have a global black market to sell your data. This is often done across the so called "Dark Web"; which is a dank little corner of the web where tracing activity is extremely difficult. Facial recognition technology and social networks like Facebook mean that your digital image is no longer secure. Every snap pic of your dinner from your favorite restaurant, to graduation pics, even those risqué pics you sent to your boyfriend only once, are all now part of the digital universe. It has even gotten to the point where fingerprints and biometric data can be lifted directly from a photo image. You no longer have the expectation of privacy for any picture whatsoever.

Major companies actually do a pretty good job of securing their corporate data within their four walls. Unfortunately, these same companies outsource significant volumes of their data to third and fourth parties located around the world. The smaller outsourced companies seldom have the same rigorous security measures that the major companies have. Bad guys know about this vulnerability too. This is specifically why the bad guys focus their efforts on the softer targets. This is where the bulk of SSN, credit card, and medical information are actually compromised. I have seen statistics that an SSN or credit card number may be sold for $.50 per record on the Dark Web. Compare this to health records, which can often fetch $20 or more per record. The health records are traded at a higher value because they are much easier to commoditize for the crooks via prescriptions.

If the everyday "Joe" didn't have enough to worry about, we need to consider good old fashion corporate greed. Specifically through ridiculously lengthy terms of acceptance contracts, which even lawyers have difficulty getting through, corporations secure the rights to sell your digital footprint to the highest bidder. Recently internet providers have secured the right to sell your browsing history. Online search engines routinely sell your search history, as well as, pump targeted ads directly to your browser. Dish and cable TV networks sell your viewing preferences. And all other retail companies can sell your purchasing history, as well as personal data. Where exactly is your privacy in all of this? Today your privacy simply no longer exists.

What should we do to combat this loss of privacy? Frankly, we cannot turn back technology, which significantly limits our options. We can and should take regulatory measures which will make compromising privacy more difficult. Specifically we can require that ALL consumer data maintained by a company is fully encrypted. This would raise enormous cost to corporations to comply with this requirement as simply they only do it on a very limited basis today. We also should require all 3rd, 4th, and n^{th} party outsource companies to likewise encrypt every bit and byte of information in their possession during both storage and transmission.

In addition to these measures, our Congress should enact rules prohibiting any and all sales of consumer data to any other company regardless of the data source or corporate relationship. Lastly, I would recommend that all citizens routinely check their credit reports for suspicious and fraudulent items on a monthly basis. On a yearly basis, I would recommend requesting & reissuing all new Credit & Debit cards for everyone in your family. Welcome to the new digital norm.

Rossiyskaya Federatsiya

Ah, the ever pungent aroma of stewed borscht and gratuitous vodka, Mother Russia. For most of the 20th Century, the United States and the former U.S.S.R. were perilously locked in a game of nuclear one-upmanship. The Cold War held all of humanity in the balance for decades. Most Americans believe that we ultimately triumphed in the Cold War during the 1980's ending the threat. Unfortunately, it's not as clear-cut as that.

After World War II, the US and the USSR were embroiled in an ideological race for global supremacy. This race took place in every imaginable corner of the world; space, geopolitical, sports, harvests, oil, technology, and of course weapons of mass destruction. From Sputnik, man's first step on the moon, the wars of North Korea and Vietnam, "Ich bin ein Berliner", Spassky and Fischer, and of course thousands upon thousands of nuclear warheads pointed at each other ensuring complete mutual annihilation; was all the result of our Cold War with the USSR. In the 1980's America under committed leadership simply out spent the USSR into complete financial collapse. Under the communist market system the USSR was incapable of financially matching the military arms spending of the United States, who enjoyed a more efficient free market capitalist system. Everyone remembers the famous challenge from our president "Mr. Gorbachev tear down this wall". Remarkably in November 1989 the Berlin wall, the irrefutable defining symbol of the Cold War, fell by popular uprising.

Soon after this historic event, the entire Soviet edifice came crumbling down. Over the next few years no less than ten former Warsaw Pact members joined the US-led NATO alliance, including the Czech Republic, Bulgaria, Poland, Hungary, Romania, and several others implementing various forms of Democracy. In addition, 15 independent countries emerged after the USSR collapse. These former soviet countries included the Ukraine, Belarus, Lithuania, Latvia, Armenia, Uzbekistan, and several others, many of which move towards democratization. The surviving Russian Federation (aka. Russia) was literally a fraction of the former USSR in territorial boundaries, population, and global influence. This new reality was horribly humiliating to many individuals, especially for the Russian nationalist, who grew up under the ever present hammer and sickle of the USSR flag.

The collapse of the Soviet Union, independence of several Soviet regions, and democratization of both former Soviet states and allies was a historic opportunity that the United States failed to successfully capitalize. Once the Soviet Union collapsed, America should have aggressively moved to stabilize the fledgling democracies and their markets; much like we did after World War II with West Germany and Japan. Instead of assisting and stabilizing these new countries, America largely turned our back on the newly found countries, leaving them to their own demise while we proudly strutted around as the victors of the Cold War. Without stabilization of both the new governments and monetary systems by the US, the new countries floundered both politically and economically. Power vacuums were soon created across the old USSR and its former sphere of influence.

From this humiliating and chaotic environment, the stage was set for the rise to power of Vladimir Vladimirovich Putin. He claimed the Russian Presidency through a series of questionable elections. But more accurately runs Russia not as a President elected by the will of the people, but rather a despot who the people fear. Though, this isn't obvious if you consider his supposed recent 83% approval rating. Rest assured approval ratings can be very misleading. For Example, on August 19, 1934 the New York Times published a poll with the heading *"Hitler Endorsed by 9 to 1 in Poll on his Dictatorship..."* In addition, Saddam Hussein enjoyed a whopping 90% approval rating. Funny, how dictators always get good popularity ratings, when the threat of death or torture is applied. The Russian people fear Putin for good reason, according to the Washington Post (March 23, 2017) at least ten outspoken political opponents of Putin have wound up mysteriously shot or poisoned. Coincidental, huh? Today Russia operates more as an Oligarchy by a handful of extremely wealthy cronies with Putin calling the shots, as opposed to a true Democracy.

Vlad is an interesting fella for sure. Now I'm not any type of Psychiatrist, Psychologist, Counselor, Head-Shrink or even a bartender, so take my thoughts on what makes Putin tick with a grain of salt. It's purely from observation, but it's very important to understand. Putin was born in Leningrad (now St. Petersburg), USSR in 1952 soon after WWII. His parent's survived the incredibly brutal and savage 2 ½ year siege of Leningrad by the Nazi Army where 800,000 civilians died. A siege so brutal, it wrought unspeakable deprivation, freezing, starvation, and even cannibalism of both the living and dead; a grizzly and gruesome reality by any measure. Undoubtedly, his parents first hand suffering and ordeals a few years earlier had to have influenced his household and early childhood. It is not difficult to understand how socio-pathetic tendencies could develop in such an environment. In addition to this stark upbringing, it's important to note that Putin was the only child of three in his family that survived. Again, survival is a critical component to understanding Putin.

Putin grew up during the height of the Cold War on a steady diet of Soviet propaganda and self-professed world supremacy. He was only five years old when Sputnik took flight, seven when Castro took over Cuba, nine when America unsuccessfully attempted the Bay of Pigs and the Berlin Wall was erected, ten during the Cuban missile crisis, and not quite seventeen when Apollo landed the first man on the moon.

Obviously this was a very formidable time in both world history and Putin's life. When he was little more than twenty-three, he joined the infamous KGB (Komitet Gosudarstvennoy Bezopasnosti – USSR's Secret Police), where he learned the importance of Intelligence and espionage, as well as how to effectively neutralize critics, opposition, and dissenters. Although Putin served in the KGB reaching the rank of Colonel, he was never a devout communist, but rather more of a Russian Nationalist.

During the 1980's, the world witnessed Russia's influence virtually emasculated with the revolution of several communist states, the fall of the Berlin Wall, the reunification of Germany, the collapse of the USSR, and the disintegration of the Warsaw Pact. Putin quickly resigned his post with the KGB during the Russian Coup d'état joining the revolution and shunned his communist ties. He swiftly rose through the post-Soviet Political landscape to the position of Prime Minister and ultimately multiple terms of President.

Putin clearly sees himself, as a defender and protector of Mother Russia. In reality, he demonstrates tendencies of narcissism, grandiosity, and Napoleon Complex with a ruthless sociopathic tendency towards eliminating opposition by any means. Also he is not above accumulating wealth, through both legal and illicit means (e.g. Sochi Olympic Games). This is possibly in an attempt to quench the deprivation of his early childhood.

To that end, he desperately seeks to restore Russia's influence, prior territories, and global prestige while increasing his own personal wealth. These are his motivators. He really isn't that complex to understand. Unfortunately, Putin sees the

United States as a direct competitor of Russia and an obstacle to renewed global dominance. In his view, that which is bad for America must be good for Russia. He pursues this relentlessly.

He is certainly not a dumb man. He does not want a military confrontation with America, which likely would not end well for Mr. Putin. Nonetheless, he does wish to undermine and attack America and our Allies in the hopes of increasing Russia's prestige and influence in the world. Please note, nothing is decided within Russia without Putin's direct knowledge, support, and approval. For better or worse if you are dealing with Russia, you are dealing with Putin. In pursuit of his goals he has attempted to weaken NATO members, sow dissent and disinformation in the United States, prop-up Terroristic States (e.g. Syria), as well as directly expand Russian territory though Military force against weaker neighbors (e.g. Crimea and Ukraine). He is methodically attacking American influence.

Recently seventeen US Intelligence Agencies, **ALL** concurred that Russia hacked and extensively meddled in our Presidential election. This is NOT up for debate, it's a fact. Personally, I have absolute confidence in the insight and patriotism of our men and women within our Intelligence Agencies. I have no doubt that they are absolutely correct in their judgement. In addition, it now appears that Russia attempted the same nefarious games in both France and British elections; undermining the democratic process in multiple western countries. As I mentioned earlier, nothing happens in Russia without Putin's blessing. So we must conclude that Putin was ultimately responsible for the attack on our Democracy.

My only issue with our America Intelligence Agencies is not with the veracity or accuracy of their findings and conclusion, but rather with the generous characterization that Russia "interfered" or "meddled" in our election. Those are very softball terms in my book. I believe Russia engaged in no less than espionage, sabotage of our most fundamental rights, and a nefarious act of war against our country. They must pay.

As we all learned on the playground when we were kids, the only way to deal with a bully is to punch them squarely in the nose. Russia is a large country attempting to flex its muscles. We need to once again take them down to size. The old adage "how do you eat an elephant" comes to mind. The answer of course is "one bite at a time". We need to revise our Russian strategy to win a New Cold War, which we are undoubtedly now in and will remain until Putin capitulates.

As part of our New Cold War Strategy, there are several things we must do straightaway to deal with illegal Russian aggression. First and foremost, we must strengthen NATO members, their economies, and military deterrents. Immediately and unequivocally, we must fully endorse NATO Article 5 (Collective Defense) and remove any doubt whatsoever that we are not fully committed to the greatest alliance in history. Next all NATO nations need to proactively reach out, assist, stabilize and aid ALL the former USSR nations that are now independent and reject Russia imperial encroachment and influence. Perhaps the most important of these is Ukraine, Poland, and Uzbekistan which we must provide significant arms that they can independently stand against Russian aggression.

In addition to strengthening and extending our Strategic Alliances, we need to impose wide scale financial sanctions and ensure our Allies follow suit on both Russia and Russian Leadership. Freeze Russian assets in our financial systems. Evict all Russian embassy or government workers/contractors from US soil. Park the "3rd Herd" on Russia's doorstep with plenty of fuel and ammo, while positioning several Air Craft Carriers and Nuclear Subs on their immediate coast. In addition, we need to engage in aggressive and well-coordinated cyber-attacks of our own, targeting Russian infrastructure, industry, energy, transportation, and financial markets with the intent to financially cripple Russia. If idle hands are the devil's workshop, we need to ensure Mr. Putin is a very busy little boy.

Personally I would like Russia to act like a responsible global citizen to help proactively resolve both North Korea and Syria, as well as other issues around the world like Human Rights and Environmental concerns. I believe extreme heightened pressure applied to both Russia and Putin directly, will help them see the light, eventually. We need to exercise and apply these pressures with the expressed goal of punishing Russia and Putin for the egregious espionage, as well as, moving them in a constructive and proactive direction. Time will tell.

Final word on Russia, there has been a lot of noise lately in the news about US Citizens possibly colluding with Russia to hack our elections, share opposition research, obstruct justice, and sow political dissent. Personally, I don't believe Russian cyber-intelligence groups needed anyone's outside technical help to hack the US elections. Putin approved it. They knew exactly what they were doing and more importantly how to do it. Even so, I am far less convinced that US Political candidates, their campaigns, or their surrogates may have had advanced knowledge of the Russian planned cyber-attacks without reporting it, shared highly sensitive opposition research, or conspired to obstruct the resulting investigation. To me this would be as serious as having advanced knowledge of either Pearl Harbor or 9/11 and not reporting it.

Beyond potential advanced knowledge, I am more than a little suspicious that folks may have coordinated with Russia publishing leaked information on WikiLeaks for maximum timing and political gain. Good News, I believe the checks and balances of our Democracy are actually working and the news media, especially The Post and NY Times (shout out!), are doing a superior effort uncovering the truth. As a result, the possibility of any American collusion is being closely scrutinized. I am not casting a stone that anyone did or did not collude with Russia on the known hacking of the US Election or sharing opposition research data. But let me be perfectly clear, if **ANY** American is found guilty of assisting the Russians with undermining our Democracy, I believe this would constitute a Treasonous Act. The United States Code 18 U.S.C. § 2381 states:

> *"Whoever, owing allegiance to the United States, levies war against them or adheres to their enemies, giving them aid and comfort within the United States or elsewhere, **is guilty of treason and shall suffer death**, or shall be imprisoned not less than five years and fined under this title but not less than $10,000; and shall be incapable of holding any office under the United States."*

Robert Marks

Social Security

Social Security is more than just an economic security net for our senior citizens. Today Social Security is actually an irreplaceable lifeline for millions of our elderly. Without the benefits of Social Security, undoubtedly millions would struggle and potentially perish. It is little wonder that any discussion related to changing social security is met with immediate and fervent resistance. However, today we must make changes.

Unfortunately, our current Social Security Trust Fund is quickly heading towards default and is projected to be exhausted by 2034. There are several contributing factors which has caused this reality. First and foremost, folks are simply living longer. In 1935 when Social Security was enacted, the average life expectancy in America was sixty-one. Today life expectancy in the US is approaching eighty. So folks are now living much longer and receiving benefits for a longer time. Our population has definitely aged. As a result, we have less folks earning and contributing to Social Security, while we have more depending on the benefits. Both issues combined have caused an untenable situation where the Social Security Trust will soon be depleted. Accordingly, we must take corrective action today to ensure its solvency, while preserving our commitment to the most vulnerable in our society.

We basically have only two options at hand to address the Social Security insolvency. These options are a) increase the contribution rate thus raising more money or b) decrease the benefit payables thus reducing the expense. There is a 3rd option, which I feel is asinine and not worthy of legitimate discussion. That option being to divide the existing fund and disburse it to citizens so they could "invest themselves" under a privatized system. The individuals who push this idea are typically Bankers, Brokers, and Hedge Fund Executives who are frothing to get their greedy little paws on your money. They literally could care less if a senior citizen lives or dies.

So let's focus our efforts on the two legitimate options to rescue Social Security, ignoring the greedy callous bankers. Remember guys, I am a 53 year old ordinary guy. I am certainly not rich or even well off. As most senior Americans my parents and in-laws (now past) were completely dependent on Social Security for income. So too were my grandparents. I truly understand the importance of preserving Social Security. Please know anything I am saying regarding this topic would directly impact my own pocketbook, my future security, and that of my children. By both raising revenues and cutting costs, we can stabilize Social Security with $150 Billion annually additional net funding. The following approach outlines the strategy. All numbers would have to be scored by GAO/CBO.

First off, we need to increase revenues into Social Security. The approach below would not affect most Americans, but could provide significant additional funding for the program. Unknown to most Americans, as of 2017 we actually have a salary cap of $127,200; above which folks are exempted from paying into Social Security. You heard me, the poor and middle class are disproportionately paying the bulk of the bill for Social Security. If an individual makes $2 million in salary, they are **ONLY** paying taxes for Social Security on the first $127,200. Not only do we need to eliminate this ceiling salary cap altogether to ensure the wealthy are actually paying their share; but we need to go a step further and raise the current rate from 7.3% to 8.5% for all annual income above $200,000.

These measures will help raise additional needed funding for Social Security. As I mentioned, these changes will not affect

90% of US citizens, but will rightly affect the wealthiest 10% earners and ensure they are indeed paying their **FAIR** share.

So now let's turn our focus to reducing annual outlay of Social Security expenses. My goal is to not affect folks currently depending on Social Security benefits, whatsoever. Today, if you were born prior to 1970 your full benefits retirement age is sixty-seven. I believe the full benefit age should be increased to:

Birth Year	Qualified Full Benefits Age
--------------------	------------------
Before 1954	66
Between 1954 - 1960	between 66 and 67
1960 - 1970	67
1970 - 2000	70
After 2000	72

As our life expectancy continues to increase, we should likewise adjust the age to qualify for Full Benefits. In doing this we will significantly reduce future outlays.

Social Security was never meant as a convenient Club-Med Travel coupon for the wealthy, but rather as a necessary safety net for our most vulnerable to ensure these individuals are afforded the very basics of a dignified life. I am quite sure that I will hear screaming from the well-manicured mansions in Bellaire on this one, but "Jimmy Crack Corn and I don't care!" I want to ensure that only those individuals truly needing this benefit actually receive it. Social Security is a critical lifeline to our elderly citizens. We must preserve it. Currently federal pensions account for nearly 25% of our annual US Budget. This translates to just over $1 Trillion annually. The largest portion of this is Social Security followed by Military and Federal employee pensions.

I would like to establish an annual household income cap of $200,000 for all Federal Pensions. This means that Federal pensions would only be paid until the Total Household Income equaled $200,000 but not a penny more. Any federal pension monies, which would cause the household income to exceed $200,000 would not be paid for that year. Again this is a cost saving measure which will not affect the vast majority of US Citizens receiving Social Security or other Federal Pensions. I know I can hear the whining today, "That's unfair; I paid into the system all those years... pay it back". That is certainly true, however, the essence and purpose of Social Security was to protect our most vulnerable citizens, and not the lifestyle of the jet-setting rich and famous.

Syria

Syria's apocalyptic descent into chaos and madness began during the Pro-democracy Arab Spring uprisings of 2011. Initially pro-democracy youth protests erupted in March 2011, as they did in many Arab nations. The Syrian protests quickly spiraled out of control when Syrian President Bashar al-Assad ruthlessly cracked down on the uprisings. Assad's regime arrested and tortured many of the youths that were involved in the uprising. This prompted further and wider protest across Syria. Assad's security forces attempted to quickly and mercilessly crush all protest by opening fire on demonstrators. As a result, soon a full blown civil war erupted between Syrians seeking Assad's immediate removal and loyalist trying to prop Assad's regime up. Over the following years this civil war has cost hundreds of thousands innocent Syrian lives and forced another eleven million others to flee their homes.

In 2012 after just a year of conflict, the United Nations Secretary General and Nobel Peace Laureate Kofi Annan along with the Arab League proposed a very reasonable (6) Point Peace Plan for Syria. This plan was purportedly accepted by Bashar al-Assad at the time. A brief synopsis is below:

(1) Commit to work with the Envoy in an inclusive Syrian-led political process to address the legitimate aspirations and concerns of the Syrian people...

(2) Commit to stop the fighting and achieve urgently an effective United Nations supervised cessation of armed violence in all its forms by all parties to protect civilians and stabilise the country...

(3) Ensure timely provision of humanitarian assistance to all areas affected by the fighting...

(4) Intensify the pace and scale of release of arbitrarily detained persons, including especially vulnerable categories of persons, and persons involved in peaceful political activities...

(5) Ensure freedom of movement throughout the country for journalists...

(6) Respect freedom of association and the right to demonstrate peacefully as legally guaranteed.

Syria

The well intentioned UN Peace effort quickly failed amongst United States demand that Syrian President Assad would step down, Russia and China's repeated vetoing of pertinent UN Security Council Resolutions, and most importantly Syria's refusal to implement the full peace plan. As a result Mr. Annan resigned on August 2, 2012 and extinguished the last legitimate opportunity for peace in the past five years. The UN capitulated.

The Syrian civil war has since escalated and became infinitely more complex when the internal conflict was regionalized with four distinct groups now fighting in Syria. The four groups now vying for control are a) Assad's Shia Sect of Islam b) Sunni Sect of Islam, c) the Kurds (Sunni) and the d) ISIS Terrorist Group. Each of these different groups is pursuing their own agendas, while civilians are caught in the crossfire.

Along the religious lines of Shiite vs Sunni, various neighboring states of Syria began pouring in resources in support of one side or the other. Instead of merely a Civil War against the brutal dictatorship of Assad, the conflict became a proxy war between the Shia Alawite Sect of Islam supporting Assad and the Sunni Sect in opposition. Assad has received considerable financial support from Iran and Lebanon's Hezbollah movement, which are both Shiite. In addition Assad received considerable military assistance, equipment, and advisors from Putin's Russia. The Sunni opposition against Assad received backing from the Sunni countries of Turkey, Saudi Arabia, Qatar and Jordan with limited military assistance from the US, France, and the UK. ISIS terrorists are pursuing the establishment of a caliphate, a religious state, in both Syria and IRAQ. The thirty-five million Kurds (in Northern Syria, Iraq, Turkey and Iran) are seeking the realization of an independent state, which was promised at the end of WWI. What we are left with in Syria is a multi-dimensional hornet's nest and enormous humanitarian crisis, which has resulted in countless deaths, suffering, and mass refugee migrations.

A little background to level set Russia's involvement. Russia is supporting the Assad regime for multiple non-religious reasons. Syria has long been a major buyer of Russian and Soviet weapons. Russia has considerable direct financial investments in Syria. In addition, Russia has an important and highly vulnerable naval base on the Mediterranean Sea in Tartus, Syria. Like many other countries worldwide, Russia is threatened by and wants to defeat the ISIS terrorist within Syria. Also not to be under estimated, Putin seeks to maintain a global sphere of influence with Russia's long-time ally, Syria. Specifically, Putin seeks to undermine U.S. influence in the middle-east and elsewhere.

Syria

It has been estimated to date, the death count in the Syrian Civil War is 470,000 with 55,000 of those being children. In an effort to cling to power, Assad has heartlessly used chemical weapons and nerve gas on his own civilians without mercy. As a result, Assad has rightly been labeled a war criminal for his use of chemical and nerve weapons. The level of absolute suffering in Syria was well articulated during a UN Security Council session in December 2016, the UN's humanitarian chief Stephen O'Brien, said there were now almost 1 million Syrians living under siege. He went on to say:

> *"Horror is now usual – it is a level of violence and destruction that the world appears to consider normal for Syria and normal for the Syrian people. Month after month I have reported to this council that the level of depravity inflicted upon the Syrian people cannot sink lower, only to return the following month with hideous and, with shocking disbelief, new reports of ever-worsening human suffering,"*

So what can we do to end the suffering and humanitarian crisis in Syria? Given the multi-dimensional nature of simply having so many different hostile combatants in a small region all vying for power, I do not believe it serves American interest to put our Son's and Daughter's boots on the ground in Syria. However as a compassionate people, we cannot turn our back on the continued suffering and carnage of innocent civilians.

I would favor a negotiated, brokered, Geo-Political peace deal between the four major state sponsors and players in the Syrian conflict, expressly not including any direct combatants. The countries we would need to engage for a brokered peace are Turkey, Russia, Iran, and the United States. All of these countries have been contributing both financially and militarily to various sides in the conflict and prolonging the carnage.

The goal of the brokered peace would be to partition Syria into multiple "safe zones" and separate the various combatants' open hostilities and direct engagement. The partitions would be drawn along ethnic and religious lines where disenfranchised populations could safely coalesce. Before we can discuss lasting peace in the area, we first must stop the carnage and enable global aid. The natural partitions that make sense would be a) Shia Alawite Sect b) Sunni Sect, c) Kurds, and d) Turks.

An important topic that America may have to table temporarily, which can be addressed in the future after hostilities have ceased, is demanding Assad's immediate removal from the presumed Shia Alawite partition. Trust me I

Syria

don't like this anymore than anyone else. However, our primary focus should be to immediately stop the killing and stabilize the region for no other reason than purely humanitarian, saving innocent lives, and stopping the flow of refugees. As reported by Reuters (3/15/2017) Andrew Tabler, a Syria specialist at the Washington Institute for Near East Policy, observed:

> *"I don't see Russia or Iran asking him (Assad) to step down, but we do have to prepare for an eventuality in this volatile environment that Assad may be targeted for assassination because of how much of a barrier he is to a settlement - him personally... If you're Iran and Russia and you know Assad's manpower limitations and political rigidity you have a problem," says Tabler. "You have to cut a deal so that Iran and Russia don't have to surge troops into Syria, which is their dilemma."*

The reason I believe a partition solution may work, at least on the interim, is the fact that all sides have fought themselves to exhaustion. Russia is interested in protecting her naval port in Tartus, Turkey and Iran wish to protect their aligned religious populations, the Kurds seek self-rule, and all of the major State Players want to avoid huge additional cost.

Robert Marks

Term Limits

A lifelong politician is a lot like a lifelong canker sore, it just ain't a pretty sight. Term limits is one of those things in our Democracy that we almost got right. As far back as the Constitutional Convention of 1787, there was serious debate over limiting terms. Even so, this didn't happen until 1947 when Congress finally approved the 22nd Amendment, which was subsequently ratified by the states (4) years later. The reason I say "almost" got right is the fact that the 22nd Amendment ONLY limits the number of terms a President can serve, expressly:

"No person shall be elected to the office of the President more than twice, and no person who has held the office of President, or acted as President, for more than two years of a term to which some other person was elected President shall be elected to the office of President more than once."

The problem was that our ever wily, clever, and self-serving members of Congress wanted to limit the Presidents job, but NOT their own cushy situation. In our two hundred plus year history, we have only had one single president who has served a little more than twelve years. It's important to note that during that same timeframe we have literally had several hundred Congressmen and Senators who have served more than twelve years. Our longest-serving member of Congress was on Capitol Hill a whopping fifty-nine years. That's nearly a lifetime. Today we have an incredible nineteen current members of Congress/Senate that have served in excess of thirty-five years each and nearly eighty current members serving more than twenty years each. Wonder why things never change in Washington D.C.? The 19th Century British historian and moralist, Lord Acton warned in 1887:

> *"Power tends to corrupt, and absolute power corrupts absolutely. Great men are almost always bad men."*

When you have an elected official squatting on power for a lifetime, the public is not being served, but rather the politician is serving themselves.

We should take Lord Acton's warning to heart. No elected official in a Democracy should serve more than twelve years, before relinquishing their office. Heck it could be argued that some of our Members of Congress shouldn't serve a single year, let alone twelve. But that is a horse of a different color. Today it is far too easy for our Congress to be influenced by an endless sea of financial contributions, enticements, and entitlements continually served up by deep-pocketed Lobbyist and PACs. For the most part the members are bought once and the Lobbyist/PACs can rest assured that they "own" their vote on matters of consequence for the entirety of their longevity in Congress with occasional donations to re-elections campaigns.

Recent Gallup polls suggest that 74% of Americans disapprove of how Congress is handling their job. Like most Americans, I have a very tarnished view of our Congress. Given our poor view of Congress, it seems reasonable that we should limit how long these individuals are permitted to serve in their role. I have heard the argument that it can take up to ten years for Members of Congress to acclimate to Washington D.C., the process of governing, and the Office they have been elected to. Horse poop! If the elected official is literate, it wouldn't take a day to read a proposed Bill or Law and cast their vote in the best interest of their constituents. It "may" take a little longer to write/author their first bill, but still not ten years. I surmise what takes ten years to acclimate, is actually the time needed to figure out how best to line their pockets and benefit financially. And that specifically is what we need to limit with terms.

While a new Constitutional Amendment limiting the terms of Congress members to twelve years is desperately needed to restore the confidence of the American people, I doubt seriously such an Amendment would ever come to pass. The reason is simple. Members of Congress largely control their own destiny on this issue and frankly gorging themselves at the public trough for decades ain't a bad gig if you can get it. As a Constitutional Amendment is unlikely today, it is also unlikely that Members of Congress will willingly step down after twelve years. It's just too financially cushy of a job to walk away from. And what would be their alternative? Hitting the pavement in search of a "real" job and schlepping to work like the rest of us, I don't believe they could handle a legitimate job.

As it stands, there is no Congressional Term Limit Amendment on the foreseeable horizon and these engorged ticks ain't likely to hop off the dog's backside by themselves. So it is up to us, the American citizens, to do the heavy lifting on this one and we really need to. Good news, we have it within our power, regardless of how much money the PACs and Lobbyist have contributed to re-elect their favorite "yes-men". The American citizens should vote all incumbents out of Office after they serve ten years if not earlier. But we all need to do it without fail. The polls show that collectively we do not like Members of Congress; however we tend to be ok with the politicians from our own neck of the woods and continually re-elect them. As a result of this voter-blind spot, we get lifelong politicians with the same old song and dance. Bring an end to it.

This is NOT a Democrat or Republican issue, but rather an American issue. I truly hope folks can set aside their party loyalties and vote out every Member of Congress, who has served more than ten years. If a Republican has served for ten years, then vote for a Democrat or vice versa. Heck, I wouldn't mind if we elected a third party candidate or an independent. Any honest, well intentioned American would be better than an incumbent who has served more than ten years. If the American voter successfully did this for a decade or so, than all the sudden a Term Limit Amendment protecting the American Citizens would become a very real possibility. Congress would have no remaining incentive to reject such an amendment.

Terrorism

Sadly terrorism and terrorist have existed as long as humanity has walked the face of the earth. It has always taken different forms across history, presented in countless ways, and with different end objectives. Nonetheless, evil has always existed in one form or another, so too has terrorism. Undoubtedly, terrorism will continue to exist into the distant future.

All of the major world religions document various acts of terrorism or offer parables and lessons addressing this scourge. Whether we're talking about the persecution of Christians being thrown to the lions, the infamous Zealot group the Sicarii, the Al-Hashshashin (the Assassin's) in the 11th century, or the Buddhist monks of Sri Lanka, religion has often been both source and target of terrorism.

Beyond religion, terrorism often takes the form of State sponsored repression. La Terreur (the Terror) occurred in the late 18th Century in France during the French Revolution. The ruling class of France at the time performed mass public executions by guillotine to hold sway over the masses. In the 20th Century Stalin deployed terror during the Great Purge when he killed over 10 million dissidents and political enemies. In addition to applying terrorism against its own population, sometimes States, like North Korea or Iran, export terrorism, technology, and techniques for profit to the highest bidder.

Likewise, race and politics are frequently the justification of terrorism, taking the form of genocide. Hitler's Holocaust, the killing fields of the Khmer Rouge, and the Bosnian Genocide in the 90's are all examples of terrorism. Race too is often the basis of political terrorism. You need look no further than the KKK's murderous rampage and lynchings following the end of the Civil War to present day, Apartheid in South Africa, the Black Panthers, or the Munich Massacre of Israeli athletes at the hands of the Palestinian group, Black September.

Terrorism is clearly an Omni-present reality throughout humanity and our history. We cannot, nor should we, ascribe or blame any certain race, ethnicity, or religion with the totality of terroristic intent. It is too often convenient and politically expedient to do this precisely; to label one group as the perpetrator of all terrorism. This is not only wrong, but frankly a simple minded excuse, political prop, and rationalization to an infinitely complex problem, specifically why do humans do what they do? I prefer to view terrorism more holistically as a battle of Good vs Evil. Perhaps this isn't' right, but it is nearly the only way I can understand and place it into context. As terrorism can assume the form of race, religion, ethnicity, or political agenda, it is an ever morphing and nebulous enemy. There simply is not one single group in the world that we can blame for terrorism.

The reason I cast terrorism as a battle of Good versus Evil, is the fact that at the root of all terrorism is a profound hatred. You could overlay any reasoning or explanation of race, religion, ethnicity, or politics as the justification for why the terrorist attack was taken. However, hatred is fundamentally always at the heart of any of these actions; thus the battle of Good vs Evil. This battle is as old as time.

If hatred is the root cause of terrorism, and I believe it is, then the antidote to hatred is love, generosity, and compassion. Just as darkness recedes from light, terrorism cannot further hatred in the presence of love. Evil cannot exist in the presence of Good. I realize this approach is much harder to practice then merely preach. If your community or loved ones are directly impacted by a terroristic act, it is human nature to seek revenge against the perceived group sponsoring the terroristic act and quickly strike back. Although this is human nature, we cannot allow our own hearts to be filled with hatred towards others. The moment that we fill our heart with similar hatred is the instant that the terrorists have succeeded in their macabre goals. Unknowingly, we have justified the original heinous act simply by hating them back. We have also furthered their recruiting efforts to perpetuate similar acts by others, while continuing the never ending cycle of hatred and violence.

Though painfully difficult, individually we must resist the temptation of filling our hearts with consuming hatred in response to a terrorist act. Manchester, Boston, and New York are but a few sterling examples of communities who came together with open hearts and embraced one another with strength, resolve, and love. These are outstanding illustrations of how our communities should react to terrorist acts. While we should react with love and generosity in our hearts, we must resist knee-jerk, ill placed reactionary laws which limit our freedoms or discriminate against others. Ignore the self-promoting politician seeking to exploit our raw emotions.

Our country should, however, take any/all proactive steps to block, undermine, disrupt, and foil terroristic acts which pose an imminent threat to our citizens whether domestic or abroad. The proactive steps of our government can and should leverage any multitude of techniques from intelligence, cyber, financial, and military. If we have credible evidence to engage a pre-emptive strike to neutralize a potential terrorist threat on any of these fronts, we should execute it without haste. This would include drone hunting, Special Forces, Guided Missiles, cyber jamming, seizure of assets, or even Military force.

While I am fully confident in the capabilities of the US intelligence community, law enforcement, and our military to successfully carry out and affect counterterrorist measures, we must temper our expectations with the reality that we may not always be successful. The United States counterterrorist abilities and intelligence network truly are 2nd to none in the world, even so, terrorist only have to be lucky once. Sadly, it is inevitable that we will experience other despicable cowardly acts in the future. While unsettling, this is foreseeable given the stark legacy of terrorism in humanity's history. When it does occur, we cannot live in fear or hatred. How we as a nation and people react to these nefarious trials and tribulations will greatly define our inevitable victory or defeat over hatred.

Robert Marks

Transportation & Infrastructure

Once the very envy of the world; the infrastructure of the United States is quite literally collapsing around us. After decades of political dysfunction and frankly dereliction, the infrastructure in United States has been widely ignored. Over the years always tight tax dollars have been redirected away from the ever dull maintenance of our infrastructure and applied towards higher profile projects that could return political capital. Today the entire infrastructure footprint of the United States is in woeful need of repair, as politicians continually kick the proverbial can down the road instead of dealing with the issues. Across America and our entire infrastructure systems has been seriously affected by the lack of ongoing maintenance, repair, and upgrades.

So bad is our infrastructure, the American Society of Civil Engineers (ASCE) issued its annual review (Mar 2017) of our country's vital infrastructure assessing a grade of D+. The report highlighted the US infrastructure needs over the next 10 years across our entire system and broke down these needs by cost into two categories:

a) Total Funds Needed to perform ALL repairs
b) Amounts Currently Funded

The difference between these two numbers represents the monies that are required to repair our infrastructure, but simply are not available. Meaning we don't have the money ear marked or allocated to do these repairs. We're not talking about nickel and dime insignificant repairs. The infrastructure that needs to be repaired includes major projects such as: dams, bridges, highways, rail, water and wastewater, electricity, ports, airports, schools, among others.

It's important to remember that a significant portion of our current US infrastructure was actually built nearly ninety years ago during the Great Depression. At the time these work projects were initiated by the federal government to not only address critical infrastructure needs, but also as an economic stimulus and a means to lower unemployment. It is very impressive when you look at some of the infrastructure projects that are instantly recognizable today like the Triborough Bridge, the Lincoln Tunnel, the Overseas Highway connecting Miami to Key West, LaGuardia Airport, the grand Coulee Dam, and of course the Hoover Dam just to mention a few.

Based on the ASCE 2017 vital infrastructure review, the following are the additional monies needed to perform key repairs in the next 10 years with no funding currently available:

Key Repairs Needed	Estimates not Funded
Streets, Roads	$1.1 Trillion
Electricity	$177 Billion
Schools	$66 Billion
Water	$105 Billion
Levees	$70 Billion
Dams	$40 Billion
Total of Key Repairs	$1.6 Trillion

* Above represents only key repairs, additional infrastructure repairs are also needed

Although the above numbers are estimates of needed funding for infrastructure repairs over the next decade, it is very obvious that we are considerably behind on necessary maintenance. All the infrastructure repair needs are important, but many of them present both life and safety concerns for millions of people. Examples of these hazardous and dangerous needs are bridges risking collapse, contaminated drinking water, or dams and levees which may fail.

Transportation & Infrastructure

As we have ignored the needed repairs for so many decades, it is now becoming critical that we invest in our infrastructure. Unfortunately as a country, our budget is upside down (see US Budget Section) with $20 Trillion in debt and running an annual deficit of $650 Billion. So allocating the necessary funding from the existing budget would be difficult if not impossible until we get the annual deficit under control. What we can do on the interim though would be to raise $500 Billion, which could be applied immediately towards the needed repairs on a criticality and priority basis. This would be a significant step towards the total funding needed and would actually act as an economic stimulus to spark economic growth. So where do we get the $500 Billion?

We discussed earlier that the wealthiest top 0.1% of American households now owns as much as the bottom 90% households combined. We need to both begin closing that enormous wealth disparity gap, as well as, begin making critical repairs on our infrastructure. Whether or not anyone will admit it, America has been incredibly generous to the wealthiest households, especially over the last 30 years. During that time the concentration of wealth has more than doubled. I believe that the wealthiest households in America literally owe it to America to help fix our infrastructure today.

These numbers would need to be validated by the GAO/CBO. As I understand it, American households own $94.7 Trillion with the top 5 % wealthiest households controlling 64% of this or $60.65 Trillion. That's correct; the wealthiest 5% of households in America now control 2/3's of all wealth in America. Given this reality with a one-time Infrastructure Tax assessed against the Top 5% wealthiest households in America, we could raise $500 Billion to immediately begin the urgently needed infrastructure repairs. This approach would not affect 95% of all households in America, but would affect the wealthiest top 5%, who are certainly in a financial position to easily handle the one-time assessment. Nobody would ever particularly enjoy a one-time tax being assessed against them to repair our critical infrastructure. However, our American infrastructure is in critical need of repair and currently threatens millions of lives each and every day. We must fix it.

Given the unprecedented escalation of wealth concentration in America, I believe this would be a worthwhile and considerate gesture by our wealthiest families; "taking one for the team" as it were. I understand people will label this as a "Robin Hood Plan" taking from the rich to give to the poor. But I certainly don't see it that way. I see it as the wealthiest American families pitching in to help at a time of national need.

Transportation & Infrastructure

Today we find ourselves at a fork in the economic road. What is best for America? Ask yourself in this environment with the wealth disparity between rich and poor in America at all time historic levels and $20 Trillion in Debt, what makes more real sense?

a) Giving a $Trillion tax cut to the wealthiest top 5% households benefitting only the wealthy and paid directly by significantly reduced healthcare for the lowest 90% households; furthering the wealth disparity gap.

b) Taxing the wealthiest 5% households half that amount to begin repairing our collapsing infrastructure; benefitting everyone in America and simultaneously acting as an economic growth stimulus.

Personally, I believe the answer to this question is obvious. Also, I am confident that every American in their heart knows the path we should take.

US Budget

Today, the United States National Debt is a staggering $20 Trillion. Our national debt calculates to approx. $61,500 for every man, woman, and child in America. Our debt has mushroomed in the past two decades. Nearly quadrupling in size since 1996 when our total debt was $5.2 trillion. More importantly our total debt in 1996 roughly equaled only 64% of our Annual GDP (gross domestic product), which measures the size of our economy. Our debt today actually exceeds our annual GDP, as our total debt is now 105% of GDP.

This doesn't necessarily mean that the sky is falling because our national debt is so high and exceeds the gross domestic products produced. However, make no mistake this is extremely serious. This type of high debt to GDP ratio has occurred previously in our history, notably around World War II when our debt to GDP was 114% and 119% in 1945 and 1946 respectively. None the less, we need to get a handle on this.

US Budget

Without pointing fingers at either party, during the prior two decades, there were certainly numerous events that contributed to the geometrical growth of our national debt. From 9/11 and the war on terror which included executing wars in multiple countries over many years, the banking crisis and subsequent bailout, Katrina, and the great recession all contributed significantly to the ballooning of our national debt. As of the fourth quarter 2016 the United States had a GDP of $18.87 Trillion. Our annual deficit is running around $650 Billion today. And nearly 7% of all our federal outlay goes to simply servicing the interest on our national debt.

Eliminating our annual deficit and resolving our national debt is certainly important, as it is literally mortgaging the future of our children. To reduce the debt you basically have two options a) significantly grow our GDP which in turn would increase our tax revenues or b) slash expenses and cut much needed programs. As our national debt was not created overnight, we need a long-term plan to address it and resist knee-jerk expense gouging for political theater. The TEA Party folks need to take a long deep breath and exhale on this fact. We all agree, we need to address the debt in a thoughtful manner, but we can't throw the baby out with the bath water.

Our path to address the national deficit should be slow, steady, and methodical. We have several critical economical components that must be implemented first as a foundation before we can truly evaluate expenses to be cut. First and foremost, we must immediately implement a single-payer HealthCare system with Universal Medical Coverage, as I described earlier under the HealthCare topic. I cannot stress the importance of this enough. In the current environment with runaway medical cost, our ongoing healthcare is not sustainable and does not cover all Americans.

Healthcare today accounts for nearly 28% of our annual federal budget outlay or $1.2 Trillion. Implementing the AmeriCare Universal HealthCare Coverage approach, as discussed, should be a net push to the overall budget, however all Americans would have HealthCare Coverage. The Universal Medical Coverage will cut cost through a combination of eliminating un-necessary HealthCare middle men (Insurance Companies and Lawyers) while implementing standardized universal pricing. In addition, to lowering the cost of HealthCare, the Universal Medical Coverage will raise significant revenues to offset HealthCare costs by increasing the coverage pool. All in all, it should net to a push.

Implementing standardized pricing, a dramatically simplified process without Insurance Companies and Lawyers involved, and increasing the coverage pool to all Americans will certainly make HealthCare more sustainable on a go forward basis. Additionally Universal HealthCare will improve the overall health of our citizens. This by itself will positively and significantly impact our GDP on a go forward basis, although not immediately. The overall budget impact of the AmeriCare Universal Health Coverage approach should be validated by the GAO/CBO.

Once the new Universal HealthCare system has been approved, we need to immediately implement Federal Income Tax reform as discussed earlier under that topic. We need to eliminate loopholes and tax shelters for Corporations and the rich, while simplifying and applying a fair stratified tax structure for everyone. This should generate additional net tax revenues in the neighborhood of $450 Billion annually. Note I said implement a new and fair stratified tax structure not give a trillion dollar tax break to the rich. And just to reiterate giving a massive tax break to the rich (trickle-down economics) simply does not work. Trickle-down economics does nothing but concentrate wealth in the hands of the rich and away from American households, as we have seen over the past 30 years.

Regarding military spending, currently, our annual defense spending dwarfs all other countries, as we spend annually three times more than China and eight times more than Russia. Without a doubt we have the strongest military in the world and we want to keep it that way without jeopardizing our global security. Still, we can and should reduce our annual defense spending by $200 Billion, while still out spending China's defense spend 2:1. This expense reduction would be realized with the immediately withdraw of our troops from the Pakistan and Afghanistan War Theater. This should be done expeditiously, as we currently have no viable strategic mission or purpose there; squandering both American lives and money.

The next program which should be immediately implemented is the approach for stabilizing Social Security as previously discussed. The revenue raising and expense cutting efforts should generate $150 Billion additional net funding for Social Security on an annual basis. Although this money would be additional net revenues, they would have no impact on the overall US Budget, as all associated monies would be dedicated to replenishing the Trust Fund. Nonetheless, stabilizing the Social Security Program for our most vulnerable Senior Citizens is critically important.

Another program which will not immediately benefit the overall US Budget, but will be an Economic Stimulus and grow our GDP going forward is repairing our Infrastructure. As we previously discussed, this would include a one-time Infrastructure Tax assessed against the wealthiest 5% of our households. This one-time assessment would generate $500 Billion, all of which would go towards repairing our infrastructure on a priority basis.

The only immediate expenses, we should consider adding during the first year after these programs are implemented is addressing the Opioid epidemic and Cyber Security. Both of these are threats to our National Security and both should be pursued with the highest priority. We should immediately dedicate $200 Billion towards combating Opioid and Heroin, ridding them from our streets. Another $200 Billion should be dedicated to strengthening both defensive and offensive capabilities of our Cyber Security.

Once these programs have successfully been implemented, we should permit a full calendar year to ensure the related financial cost and outcomes are truly as expected before addressing Expense Reductions. Then we should address our expenses prudently. Our goal should be to reduce budgetary outlays by 6% annually.

Robert Marks

Young Americans

Be the Difference

Be the Change

Be all of our great Tomorrows, Today

Every new generation in history has altered and modified society's direction. Whether it was the Peace Protests, school age kids tuning into Elvis Presley, college kids embracing the freedom movement and civil rights in the South, or our soldiers bravely fighting on foreign soil for our country; American history has always been forged and shaped by our youth. Every young American holds all of our tomorrows in your hands today. For the foreseeable future our America, the compassion of our country, and the world we live in will largely be determined by your generation. This fact is highly comforting to me, as I personally hope for a more compassionate, accepting, and generous America for my children and grandchildren to live.

Imagine an America where there are no crosses left burning, no glass ceilings left to break, no Sandy Hooks to cry, no places of worship vandalized, no person denied whom they can love or marry, no faith ever subjugated, and no refugee turned away from our shores. Imagine an America where women are in control of their bodies and have the same earning potential as men; where children of all colors and faiths play and laugh together; where no man, woman, or child endures the hatred of prejudice. Imagine the America of tomorrow, today.

I want to challenge our young Americans to embrace your generation's promise, providence, and destiny to shape America for the better. I am wholly convinced of the infinite goodness, heart, and compassion of your generation; I have witnessed as much and been inspired by my own college age kids. Godspeed and let no one stand in your way. I will ask you to ignore the loud mouthed political shock jocks that will belittle your efforts and the backwards, entrenched, uninformed individuals who are frightened at the very prospects of changing the status quo. Take solace that your collective energy, passion, and drive will ultimately overcome all detractors and any temporary barriers placed on your path. Each and every day ask yourselves this simple question, "What have I done today to make America better and more compassionate?" Then, ***Be the Difference***!

A COMMON
MAN'S VOICE

BE THE DIFFERENCE!

ROBERT MARKS

Made in the USA
Lexington, KY
11 August 2017